HOLLY W. WHITCOMB

FEASTING WITH GOD
Adventures in Table Spirituality

United Church Press
Cleveland, Ohio

United Church Press, Cleveland, Ohio 44115
© 1996 by Holly W. Whitcomb

Grateful acknowledgment is made for use of the following:

From Kelton Cobb, "Table Blessings." Copyright 1986 Christian Century Foundation. Reprinted by permission from the March 5, 1986 issue of *The Christian Century.* ∾ Reprinted from *Meditations with Hildegard of Bingen,* by Gabrielle Uhlein. Copyright 1983 Bear & Co., Inc., P.O. Box 2860, Santa Fe, NM 87504. ∾ From Barbara Walker, *Women's Rituals* (San Francisco: Harper & Row, 1990), 88. Copyright 1990 by HarperCollins Publishers. Reprinted by permission. ∾ Judy Chicago, "Merger Poem." Copyright Judy Chicago, 1979. Reprinted by permission. ∾ Reprinted from *Meditations with Meister Eckhart,* by Matthew Fox. Copyright 1983 Bear & Co., Inc., P.O. Box 2860, Santa Fe, NM 87504. ∾ From *Dance of the Spirit* by Maria Harris. Copyright © 1989 by Maria Harris. Used by permission of Bantam Books, a division of Bantam Doubleday Dell Publishing Group, Inc. ∾ From Kay Leigh Hagan, *Prayers to the Moon: Exercises in Self-Reflection* (San Francisco: HarperSanFrancisco, 1991), 28, 80, 128, 160. Copyright 1991 by HarperCollins Publishers. Reprinted by permission. ∾ From Vincent Kavaloski, "What Is the Middle East in the Middle Of ?" *Metanoia* (summer 1991), 2. Reprinted by permission of Vincent and Jane Kavaloski. ∾ Adapted from Lucia Capacchione, *The Creative Journal,* 94, 172. Reprinted by permission of Ohio University Press/Swallow Press. ∾ Susan Cady, Marian Ronan, and Hal Taussig, *Wisdom's Feast: Sophia in Study and Celebration* (San Francisco: Harper & Row, 1989), 94, 99. Copyright 1989 by HarperCollins Publishers. Reprinted by permission. ∾ From Roger Rosenblatt, "Where in the World?" *Family Circle,* 8 June 1993, 152. Reprinted by permission of the author. ∾ Adaptation of one verse of "Sarah's Circle," by Carole Etzler Eagleheart. Reprinted by permission of the author. ∾ The lines from "i thank You God for most this amazing", copyright 1950, © 1978, 1991 by the Trustees for the E. E. Cummings Trust. Copyright © 1979 by George James Firmage, from *Complete Poems: 1904–1962* by E. E. Cummings. Edited by George J. Firmage. Reprinted by permission of Liveright Publishing Corporation. ∾ From *Life's Companion: Journal Writing as a Spiritual Quest* by Christina Baldwin. Copyright © 1990 by Christina Baldwin. Used by permission of Bantam Books, a division of Bantam Doubleday Dell Publishing Group, Inc. ∾ Poem by John Soos reprinted by permission of the author. ∾ Reprinted with permission from *Prayers for a Planetary Pilgrim* by Edward Hays, Copyright Forest of Peace Publishing, 251 Muncie Rd., Leavenworth, KS 66048-4946. ∾ "Snake Shedding" by Betsy James reprinted by permission of the author.

Unless otherwise specified, biblical quotations are from the New Revised Standard Version of the Bible, © 1989 by the Division of Christian Education of the National Council of the Churches of Christ in the U.S.A., and are used by permission. Adaptations have been made for inclusiveness.

Printed in the United States of America on acid-free paper

01   00   99   98   97   96   5   4   3   2   1

Library of Congress Cataloging-in-Publication Data
Whitcomb, Holly W. (Holly Wilson), 1953–
    Feasting with God : adventures in table spirituality / Holly W.
Whitcomb.
        p.   cm.
    Includes bibliographical references.
    ISBN 0-8298-1153-2 (alk. paper)
    1.   Cookery.   2.   Food in the Bible.   3.   Food—Religious aspects.
I. Title.
TX652.W429   1996
641.5—dc20
                                              96-34300
                                                CIP

To my ground crew:

John, David, and Kate

God gave us rain from heaven,

and fruitful seasons, filling our

hearts with food and gladness.

—Acts 14:17

CONTENTS

PART 2 CULINARY INTERLUDES

(Reflections Planned around Food, but Not Entire Feasts)

FOREWORD

Halfway through my reading of Holly Whitcomb's *Feasting with God,* I began to list people—especially close friends—with whom I wanted to share it. I listed Ann, who characteristically sends visitors home with a gift—poinsettias at Christmas; lilies at Easter—after hosting the kind of meal that makes everyone feel like family. I thought of Rosemary, whose Australian wisdom in gift-giving has made her, as is typical with Australians, a genius of hospitality. I thought of Fred, who has bonded scores of people, especially in large groups, by cooking for them on important occasions, making each meal a sacrament. I thought of Regina and Helen, at the center of innumerable sisterly vacations, whose cooking provided the festivity that centered those days for everyone lucky enough to be part of them. I remembered Bill, whose Middle Eastern roots lay at the center of the many tastes of bread to which he'd introduced me. And I recalled Sadako, the first person who'd ever led me through the contemplative pause of the Japanese tea ceremony, feeding my spirit and my soul as she did so.

I name these women and men here because Holly Whitcomb's writing evoked each of them. Not only does her brilliance in this book lift up the holiness of food, and instruct us in the many ways that we come together to feast with one another and with God—as the cooks I name above have done in my life. She also evokes the wide and wonderful variety of ways that all of us can engage in the kind of table spirituality that heralds the messianic banquet so familiar to readers of the Hebrew Bible and the New Testament, a spirituality that lies at the core of this book.

For make no mistake about it: this is a book of deep, profound, and most centrally, incarnational spirituality. Even as it celebrates and reveres our bodies and our bodies' relation with food, it points us further, directing us beyond ourselves to our vocation of care for one another and the universe. It directs us within as well, to the many ways in which we might practice fidelity to the human need to come together regularly before one another and before God, and break bread in the midst of the communities that nourish our lives.

The pattern Whitcomb uses to foster these possibilities is remarkably simple. After a brief introduction, she spins out sixteen themes that serve as points of departure for different kinds of meals/feasts/banquets. Included among these themes are such essentially human interests as creativity, rites of passage, care, wisdom, and wonder. Her giving flesh to each of these—through reflections and indescribably mouthwatering recipes, and through practical exercises and artistic expression—forms the bulk of the book, although not all of it. For dessert is still to come, and the author, by now our master teacher, concludes by offering six of what she calls "culinary interludes"—reflections planned around food, but not entire feasts. She leaves off with a practical appendix (on setting the table and creating the environment) and with an extensive and serviceable bibliography.

How does Whitcomb do it? How does she engage us, her readers, in the sacred adventures of table spirituality outlined here with such imagination? Readers will have their own responses to this question as they take up this book and then test its instructions. But certainly, each of us will be drawn in at four entry points that she makes essential to feasting with God. These entry points are welcome, biography, economy, and gratitude.

Welcome

Early on in the book, Whitcomb reminds us that the primary Welcoming One is God, who provides for us the wonders and majesty of creation, the miracle of food itself, and the privilege of being with table mates in the persons of loved ones and friends, as well as new acquaintances. But then she notes that our own role as host is an extension of God's generosity to us. She proceeds to invite us to join her at the table in order to honor the hospitality that God stirs up within us whenever we are given the opportunity to gather around a table. She follows this by teaching us how we might similarly honor our guests by suggesting innumerable practices of welcome: everything from personalized name cards, to hidden gifts within food that guests will find—a secret message within a croissant, for example—to making guests participants in the welcoming by asking them to prepare a special food that will, in turn, be a source of welcome to others joining in the feast.

Biography

Because this is a book that fosters community, the author includes places in every feast where participants may draw on their own life stories in addressing the theme of the gathering. In the feast she calls "Table of Creativity," for example, she asks guests to bring along a nonfood item that they have had some part in creating. These items are reverently placed somewhere in the room where the feast is held, and when the meal finishes, the company gathers around them in a circle, and all who wish to do so tell why they chose to bring their item. In this way, everyone is given the chance to reflect on creativity in her or his own life. Such meditation, in turn, moves to the opportunity to reflect on the creativity of everyday life: from creating a family to creating a relationship, to making a work of art, to discovering other instances that come to mind. On another occasion, guests are asked to bring a symbol or object that represents personal power in their lives. And for a still different occasion, guests are asked to bring a symbol of something they are birthing or bringing into existence in their lives right now. They are also invited to bring a food that represents their "changing tastes." Although no one is forced to speak who does not wish to, the opportunity to do so—at the meal or after the meal—affirms the importance of each one's selection and symbol, even as it affirms each one's life, particularity, and biography.

Economy

In our late-twentieth-century world, where economic issues are immediately assumed to be issues of capital and monetary investment, it sometimes comes as a surprise to be reminded that the stronger and far more ancient meaning of the word "economy" is the realm of human householding. Wendell Berry says somewhere that economy in its central meaning refers to home-making, to all the ways that human beings make, and hold, and shape the things we use; how we handle them; how we revere them; what we do with them when we've finished using them. Holly Whitcomb's book forcefully reminds me of the importance of this "home economy" as she writes reverently about the plates and pots and dishes and vessels that are part of the human table, and therefore of the human economy. True to the sacramental sensibility that pervades this book, she celebrates ordinary candles and luminaries, and the sight, sound, and smell of them; she hallows sparklers; she makes vases of pots, pans, and bowls; she suggests collections of shells or rocks or feathers as centerpieces. She sings the song of the goblet, which, though inexpensive, can transform the simplest of concoctions into something elegant. Placed in a goblet of ice water, for example, even a small slice of lemon adds panache. But it adds even more: it contributes to the beauty of the human and humane economy we find at its best in every home.

Gratitude

In a world where hunger is rampant, someone may ask, "Where does all of this celebration and feasting fit in? How can we engage in such largesse while others are in desperate need?" The short answer is, of course, that we can't, or—more accurately—we can't feast completely. Whenever we come together for table celebrations, our grace must openly be along the lines of "For those without food, grant bread; for those with bread, grant hunger for justice." And then we must go forth to proclaim justice and perform works that serve justice.

But hunger for justice does not begin with deprivation, let alone with guilt. Hunger for justice begins with gratitude, by acknowledging our minute-by-minute, hour-by-hour thanks for the gifts of the earth that become the food on our tables. God has been good to those of us whose tables are full, and to fail to acknowledge this goodness is to fail as creatures.

Moreover, it is the act of thanksgiving—"Eucharist" in the Christian dispensation—that kindles the realization that the earth-gifts meant for all do not reach all. Goodness exists, yes, but the world is not yet wholly good. So every act of gratitude is incomplete unless it issues in a sending forth to do works that will make for justice through a more equitable distribution of resources than is now ours. That is the reason, or so it seems to me, why we must pause for the feasting that centers this book—for the Sabbath about which Holly Whitcomb writes so beautifully. Out of those feasts, those Sabbath times, those Eucharists, comes the power of outrage about which she also writes—outrage that the earth's gifts are, as yet, not reaching all; outrage at the situation of the poor.

Thus, in thanking this writer for a book full of gifts—gifts that return us to the Giver—we begin with praise and thanksgiving. We also end with praise and thanksgiving. But in between, we work to create a more beautiful earth, as this woman has done in recipe after recipe, and in noting one practical implication after another. We work to create a more beautiful earth—which is to say a more just one—by coming together to the holy tables of our lives and to the great feast that is life itself. And then we spread out the gifts for all who come— again as this master chef has done—and say, "Here, this is for you. Together, let us celebrate and give thanks to the One who has summoned us to this place."

Maria Harris

PREFACE

This book is intended for those of you who are happiest when sharing intimate conversation around the dinner table. Something mystical and deeply nurturing takes place in the context of a meal shared with friends. We feed not only our bellies, but our spirits and our sense of community. We come away from the table knowing that we have shared food and the stories of our lives.

HOW TO USE THIS BOOK

This book is an invitation to use your wildest imagination to cook up good food and good company. These table gatherings are suitable for diverse groups of people: families, congregations, support groups, circles of friends, women's organizations, men's organizations, marriage enrichment or partners' groups, and intergenerational assemblies of adults and children. These feasts may take place in homes, churches, places of business, camps, conference centers, or rented halls. These feasts and culinary interludes may stand alone or be used as part of a longer workshop or retreat. The "Reflecting Together" part of each feast builds community as it provides you and your guests with provocative questions for discussion and stimulating hands-on activities.

The appendix at the end of the book, "Setting the Table and Creating the Environment," provides additional practical advice on how to get started preparing for all this good food and good company. It offers a wealth of information about setting up an attractive, convenient, and hospitable space.

Although recipes are included throughout the book, you are also encouraged to think up your own. Let the ideas in this book stimulate you, and then feel free to go where you wish. Adapt. Change. Revise. Create your own ambiance.

ACKNOWLEDGMENTS

As I wrote *Feasting with God* over a period of several years, I was aware of a mighty cloud of witnesses cheering me on.

I am grateful to the staff members of the Elm Grove, Wisconsin, Library, who helped provide me with a quiet place to write and who never tired of procuring more and more titles for me through interlibrary loan. I also thank my colleagues in the clergy who were there believing in me, passing along relevant ideas, or offering valued advice: Bob Ullman, Brenda Yeager, Sandra Graham, Tim Perkins, Ed Beers, and Michael Bausch. Thanks also to my friend Gloria Kjer, who deepened my understanding of inclusiveness. I am grateful to those published authors who took time to talk: Jacqueline McMakin, Flora Slosson Wuellner, Don Collins, Joe Juknialis, Sara Covin Juengst, and Marjorie Thompson. Thanks also to Nate Bubenzer, of Theological Book Service, who offered excellent advice about the field of religious publishing. For her astute marketing support, I am indebted to Chris Roerden. My loyal friend Agnes Barrett kept me going with her patient review of the manuscript, her helpful suggestions, and her unflagging enthusiasm. I thank my precious sister Heather for her continued faith in me as she patiently listened to me describing my progress year after year. And I thank my parents, Dave and Janis Wilson, for a wide vision of the world.

I deeply appreciate the efforts of all the staff of United Church Press, especially the skill and insight of Ed Huddleston and Martha Clark. I am also grateful to Betsy James for her illustrations. Also, many thanks go to Maria Harris, an exceptional and inspiring teacher, author, and role model, who gave of her time to write the foreword.

This manuscript could not have come to fruition without the constant support of my family and the undergirding of love and patience of my husband, John, and our children,

David and Kate. (It is ironic, however, that when my manuscript about feasting was finally finished and mailed, my eleven-year-old daughter Kate said, "Finally we can look forward to a real home-cooked meal!")

I am grateful to Julia Cameron, author of *The Artist's Way*, whose cheerleading phrases were written in the margins of all my drafts and whose belief in the creative spirit found a home in my heart.

Thanks to you all.

INTRODUCTION

MEMORIES OF TABLE SPIRITUALITY

Some of my most poignant memories of community were created around food. As I child, I loved wedding receptions with all those tall candles and little sterling bowls of mixed nuts and pastel mints. I relished Thanksgivings when all four of my grandparents could be present as we consumed the traditional turkey and pumpkin pie. As a pastor in my twenties, I was moved by the tears, laughter, and remembrances shared at funeral meals as loving relatives piled slabs of home-baked ham and mounds of potato salad onto our plates.

Just this summer, our extended family celebrated a moving baptismal feast for our niece, Caroline, who was born two and a half months prematurely and weighed only two pounds. Caroline's baptismal feast brought relatives together from all over the United States as we thanked God for her survival and the preciousness of her life.

Through the ritual of a shared meal, hospitality is extended and acquaintances become friends and companions. The word *companion* comes from the Latin: *cum,* meaning "with," and *panis,* meaning "bread." Our companions are those with whom we share meals. Our companions are those with whom we break bread. When I reflect on church services that have been the most memorable to me, they frequently revolve around food. Our church celebrates the Seder during Holy Week, and this year we invited a Hispanic congregation to join with us. I have always appreciated the sights, sounds, aromas, and intergenerational participation in the Seder: the earthy smell of fresh green parsley, the succulent scent of roast lamb, the children jumping up and down to do their readings and to ask the questions of their elders. The Seder creates a sensory memory of God's blessing and deliverance. The Jews can teach much about proclaiming a "table spirituality," having for centuries celebrated their religious feasts and holy days around the altar of the family table.

The Christian community celebrates Holy Communion, Holy Eucharist (which means in Greek "thanksgiving"). In seminary, we were taught to pour the wine with a splash and a flourish and to break the freshly baked and crusty bread with a resounding crack. In communion, our senses are stimulated as our bodies and our spirits are fed. Brother Peter Reinhart, chef and author of *Sacramental Magic in a Small Town Café* reminds us that "each of us unknowingly yearns for a communion experience every time we eat." The word *sacrament* itself is derived from root words meaning "mystery" and "sacred feast."[1] Sharing food is one of life's most primal and bonding experiences. Eating together creates community.

Many writers have observed the spiritual dimension of sharing food. Sarah Hall Maney, homemaker, poet, and author, expresses articulately the holiness of a shared meal:

> *It seems clear to me now that my mother did very sacred work in her kitchen. She presided over our dinner table and offered us a sustaining and life-giving sacrament, the product of her love and her creative energy. Such work becomes sacred, I now think, when we focus creative energy into doing something, or making something, that contributes to the health and healing, to the well-being and wholeness, of ourselves and others. So food, a meal carefully prepared, becomes a sacrament to me when I enjoy, I am nourished, I am comforted, or I am connected with others in the sharing.[2]*

M. F. K. Fisher, world-famous gastronome, observes that "there is a communion of more than our bodies when bread is broken and wine is drunk."[3] Sharon Parks, educator and writer in religion and psychology, explains:

> *We do not have to reflect very long upon the power of food to begin to see why it has such symbolic-ritual power and why meals, whether*

ordinary or special, can function as complex symbols, keys to whole patterns of relationship between ourselves and other elements of our lives—persons, things, and the source of all food, the earth itself.[4]

And a Somali proverb proclaims: *"War iyo la cuno, baa lagu nool yahay."* ("Communication and food are the things that one lives by.")

GOD AS PRESIDER AT THE BANQUET

In my personal prayer, I often vary my metaphor for the deity. One of my favorite ways to address God is as the Welcoming One. God plays the host or hostess of all creation, providing hospitality and welcoming us into the richness of the banquet of life over and over again. Matthew Fox, author and theologian, proclaims:

> *The Creator God is a gracious, an abundant, and a generous host/hostess. [God] has spread out for our delight a banquet that was twenty billion years in the making. A banquet of rivers and lakes, of rain and sunshine, of rich earth and of amazing flowers, of handsome trees and of dancing fishes, of contemplative animals and of whistling winds, of dry and wet seasons, of cold and hot climates. . . . God has declared that this banquet is "very good" and so are we, blessings ourselves, invited to the banquet.[5]*

God as the Welcoming One provides for us the wonders and majesty of creation, the miracle of food itself, as well as the privilege of other tablemates in the persons of loved ones and friends. God as the Welcoming One, our presider at the banquet, also invites us to get to know the Divine Self in the form of Jesus, the Incarnate One; certainly this intimate glimpse is hospitality in its most gracious form. Our own role as host or hostess at the table is an extension of God's own generosity to us.

Another one of my favorite ways to address God is as the Divine Chef. I love to think of God laying out the holy feast, which—as we've said before—is all of creation: the loveliness of nature, the planet, and the universe. It is worthwhile to note that chefs follow basic recipes and then set their imaginations free to create something totally original and uniquely theirs. God as our Divine Chef is always stirring up newness in the universe and in each of us. I invite you to honor the newness that God is stirring up in you and to rejoice in the opportunities you have to gather around your sacred table.

Psalm 63:5 says, "My soul is satisfied as with a rich feast, and my mouth praises you with joyful lips." May you and your guests be filled with food and gladness. May you enjoy satisfied souls while feasting with God!

GIVING THANKS

How can we eat a meal without pausing in some way to thank the One who has created us? A prayer before eating reminds us that all of life is gift. Theologian Walter Brueggemann describes these prayers as "brief sabbaths when we live by gift and know that we are strangely sustained, nurtured, and nourished." It is, he says, "worthwhile to make visible links between the *overpowering miracle of creation* and the daily *reality of food.*"[6] Tilden Edwards shares his perspective on this same theme: "Food then becomes an opportunity for *remembering* God's presence, for giving thanks, and for sharing food as heavenly manna, recalling how often meals with Jesus were occasions of revelation and calls to sharing. . . . Grace at meals is a remembrance of this pervasive divine presence for us."[7]

Table grace or prayers of blessing too often are times of rote memorization or embarrassed mumblings. The time of prayer before eating is rich with possibility. It is an occasion to gather as a community, an opportunity to lift up special events or needs in intercessory remembrance, a chance to recall that we live because God wishes that we should live.

Kelton Cobb, a Quaker carpenter, writes in *The Christian Century:*

> *The table . . . has God's fingerprints all over it. We participate in a mystery whenever we eat food. Indeed, every meal is sacramental. Through eating, death is resurrected into life. Dead fish, dead figs . . . are transformed into the living tissue of our bodies. Through some mystery brewing deep inside of us, all dead matter comes to life imprinted with our chromosomes. We receive the world's bounty as a gift from God, kill it so we can eat it, bless it, swallow it, and convert it into more life. That is an event I would call sacred—a holy occurrence.*

Cobb goes on to say that "The food we eat, and the way we handle it, may tell God a good deal. The table blessing is not simply a nice custom. It is a sacramental litany. Food and nourishment are made holy when received with a blessing."[8]

The Japanese word *Itadakimasu,* which means "I receive this food with thanks," expresses linguistically the theological sweep of thanksgiving. Mitsuko Yaguchi says, "This is the traditional way to express thanks to the farmers who work hard to produce rice, and for children to express thanks to their parents who provide their food." He continues: "We Christians can say it and think of people who work hard to make food available to us. We think of God's love working in them. We remember people who are starving or in miserable situations."[9]

Praying Our Thanks

Here are some suggestions that you and your family may find useful in varying your table grace or prayers of blessing:

∾ *Pray silently:*

Why not try a silent creation-centered prayer that encompasses the Japanese concept of Itadakimasu? All those who prepare to share the meal look carefully at the various foods set before them. Then, with eyes closed, they reflect with thanksgiving in their hearts on the journey that each item of food has made: from field or animal—nourished by God's sun and rain—to garden, or grocery, or table. One person may wish to end the time of silent thanksgiving by saying, "O God, Creator, we give you thanks."

∾ *Sing a grace:*

Choose sung graces from church or camp, or sing a verse or refrain from a favorite hymn. One of mine can be sung to the Doxology or Old Hundredth tune:
O God we thank you for this food / You give us life and call it good /
We walk with you from day to day / Be thou our Light along the way.
Amen.

∾ *Hold hands!*

∾ *Include the children:*

Ask them to offer a spontaneous prayer about what they are most thankful for that day.

∾ *Do what we call in our house "thanksgivings":*

Our children like this prayer the best. We simply go around the table saying one thing that we are especially thankful for that day. The last person to speak adds an Amen. We find that this prayer invokes a delightful intentionality in our gratitude to God. When we pray this prayer, we always end up actually thinking about the words we are saying.

PART 1

Feasts

ONE

THEME

This "feast of fat things" embodies the hopes and dreams of the messianic banquet, the feast of the realm of God. Although this feast can take place anytime, it would be particularly meaningful on New Year's Eve or New Year's Day.

PLANNING AHEAD

This feast is a potluck. Invite guests to bring their most succulent and juicy favorite foods. (See "Food as Symbol.")

UNDERSTANDING THE MESSIANIC BANQUET

The messianic banquet is an occasion on which God will break into history and the new age of realized dreams will arrive.

> *On this mountain the God of hosts will make for all peoples a feast of fat things, a feast of wine on the lees, of fat things full of marrow, of wine on the lees well refined. . . .*
>
> *God will swallow up death forever, and the Sovereign God will wipe away tears from all faces, and God will take away from all the earth the reproach of God's people; for God has spoken. (Isa. 25:6, 8)[1]*

This messianic banquet is an image often used in biblical scripture and the apocryphal writings. Some of the better-known references to an eschatological feast appear in Isaiah 25, Luke 14, and Revelation 19.

Sara Covin Juengst says, in *Breaking Bread:*

> *The messianic banquet was a familiar image in apocalyptic writings. Jesus used it to remind his disciples of that hope: they would receive not only deliverance from the bondage of sin, but joy and gladness in the unity of table where [God] is host. A feast of fat things. No more tears. No more death. These are the promises from the messianic banquet image that would be renewed each time they "broke bread together."[2]*

REFLECTING TOGETHER: OPPORTUNITIES FOR DISCUSSION

(The leader selects those topics and activities that are most appropriate for the group and for which there is time.)

Joy

The idea of the messianic banquet is sensuous and lovely and filled with joy! It ushers in the end of sorrow ("God will wipe away the tears from all faces" [Isa. 25:8]), and it announces the beginning of fulfilled hopes and celebrations.

Hildegard of Bingen, the twelfth-century mystic, has written:

Be not lax
Be not lazy in the festive service of God.[3]

Are you lax in celebrating? How is your life going in the celebration department? Are there big or small rites of passage or thanksgivings or achievements that you could be celebrating?

Are you getting your quota of joy? How might this happen? Talk with one another.

Inclusiveness

The scriptural passage quoted earlier from Isaiah 25 says: "The God of hosts will make for all peoples a feast of fat things." One of the hallmarks of the messianic banquet is that it is *for all peoples;* it is always inclusive. In the parable in Luke 14, we find God going out into the streets and bringing in the poor, the crippled, the blind, and the lame. Everyone is invited to the messianic banquet; no one is ever left out.

Think about your circle of acquaintances, colleagues, loved ones, friends. Is that circle as inclusive as it might be? Do you know persons of different backgrounds and from other cultures? Do you know persons whose lifestyles vary from yours? Are there persons you would like to befriend? Are there persons whose life stories you wish to learn? How could you be living more inclusively? Discuss.

Rules for Changing the World[4]

The messianic banquet is a feast where a past order is dismantled and a new vision is proclaimed. How would you make this world a more holistic, healthier, more humane, more just place to live?

Select a few, maybe five, of the following statements, borrowed from ritualist Barbara Walker, and go around the circle. Each person will complete the sentence. (Of course anyone is always free to pass.) Then the whole group will move to a new statement.

I would clean up . . .
I would reorganize . . .
I would tear down . . .
I would heal . . .
I would permit . . .
I would encourage . . .
I would protect . . .
I would forbid . . .
I would reward . . .
I would stop . . .
I would develop . . .[5]

Music to Create a Better World By

Play John Lennon's "Imagine," Bette Midler's "From a Distance," or other appropriate selections from your tradition. Talk together about the imagery in the songs as well as your hopes and dreams for the future.

A Vision of Heaven on Earth

Often we get stuck in our own or our society's sense of powerlessness and we forget to get in touch with our vision for a new heaven and a new earth. We forget that we have the power to dream and to make change happen. In Acts 2:17 we hear the words of the prophet Joel:

And in the last days it shall be, God declares,
that I will pour out my Spirit upon all flesh,
and your sons and your daughters shall prophesy,
and the young shall see visions,
and the old shall dream dreams.[6]

The messianic banquet is a time of dreaming dreams, a time of re-creation and restoration, a time of realized eschatology, a time of bringing heaven to earth. The following is an example of a declaration and a vision from Judy Chicago's *The Dinner Party*. Invite a guest to stand and read the vision aloud.

And then all that has divided us will merge
And then compassion will be wedded to power
And then softness will come to a world that is harsh and unkind
And then both men and women will be gentle
And then both women and men will be strong
And then no person will be subject to another's will
And then all will be rich and free and varied
And then the greed of some will give away to the needs of many
And then all will share equally in the Earth's abundance
And then all will care for the sick and the weak and the old
And then all will nourish the young
And then all will cherish life's creatures
And then all will live in harmony with each other and the Earth
And then everywhere will be called Eden once again[7]

Writing a Vision Together
Using a chalkboard, newsprint and colorful markers, or whatever writing materials are available, ask the whole circle together to write its own vision for heaven on earth. This vision may start out with the words "And then . . . ," as in *The Dinner Party,* or it may take another form. Go around the circle having every person add a line, or have anyone merely speak aloud a phrase when inspiration strikes.

FOOD AS SYMBOL

In writing about the messianic banquet referred to in Isaiah 25, Sara Covin Juengst writes:

> *What is the menu for this picnic to end all picnics? There will be "fat things" and "wine on the lees." In a land where meat was scarce, fat was highly treasured, especially the marrow in the bones. It is like saying, "There will be filet mignon and apple pie à la mode."* [8]

Guests at this feast may bring their most succulent and juicy favorite foods—maybe prime rib, fresh lobster, or new peas from the garden. Or you can try my Party Beef Tenderloin. Bring whatever makes you feel the most celebrative. Pull out all the stops. It's time to kill the fatted calf for this one!

This company dish is one version of heaven on earth; it is truly fit for a king or queen.

PARTY BEEF TENDERLOIN

1 beef tenderloin, 4–5 pounds
3 tablespoons butter, softened
5 strips bacon, cut in small pieces
1/3 cup chopped scallions
1/2 cup pine nuts
1 cup dry sherry
2 tablespoons ginger-flavored soy sauce
1 1/2 teaspoons Dijon mustard
Black pepper (to taste)

Spread meat with 3 tablespoons softened butter. Roast the tenderloin in a 400-degree oven for 25 minutes. While meat is roasting, fry together the bacon, scallions, and pine nuts. Drain bacon fat. Stir in sherry, soy sauce, mustard, and black pepper. Bring to a simmer and pour over roast, mixing with juices in pan. Roast about 25–30 minutes longer, basting several times. Don't overcook. Pour sauce over meat. Serves 10–12. This dish is good served with scalloped potatoes or rice pilaf.

Two

THEME

This feast proclaims our cocreation with God, honors our uniqueness, and helps us discover and claim our creativity.

PLANNING AHEAD

Ask guests to bring along a food item which they find particularly creative. (This food does not have to be homemade; see "Food as Symbol.") Each person is also asked to bring a non-food item that he or she feels especially good about having created.

REFLECTING TOGETHER: OPPORTUNITIES FOR DISCUSSION

(The leader selects those topics and activities that are most appropriate for the group and for which there is time.)

Creative Foods
Talk sometime during the feast about which foods were brought and why.

Creative Offerings

After the meal, gather in a circle around a table or altar on which are placed the nonfood items the guests created and brought. Go around the circle and ask each person to share: Why did you choose that particular item to bring? How did it feel to be in that process of creating?

Cocreation with God

God is the Artist with a big "A" and each of us is an artist with a little "a." What does it mean to be a cocreator with God? Discuss the following two quotations:

> *We must accept that the creative pulse within us is God's creative pulse itself.*[1]

> *To paint a picture or write a story or compose a song is an incarnational activity. The artist is a servant who is willing to be a birthgiver.*[2]

The thirteenth-century mystic Meister Eckhart wrote:

> *From all eternity*
> *God lies on a maternity bed*
> *giving birth.*
> *The essence of God is birthing.*[3]

What has God given birth to through you? How do you and God give birth together?

Enthusiasm

The word enthusiasm means literally, from the Greek, "filled with God." What activities in your life are filled with enthusiasm? How are these activities filled with God?

A Unique Combination of Gifts

You are like no one else on earth. What you have to offer is unique. Talk about the following quotation and how it relates to you and your creative gifts. How are you unique?

> *There is a vitality, a life force, an energy, a quickening, that is translated through you into action, and because there is only one of you in all time, this expression is unique. And if you block it, it will never exist through any other medium and will be lost.*[4]

What do you feel most positive about having created in your life? Share your thoughts.

As you walk through an average day, make an outline of the hours, noting all the ways in which you create throughout the day. (Remember, this can mean creating a family, a relationship, a work of art, or anything that comes to mind.) Does anything surprise you? Are you more creative than you usually give yourself credit for? Talk together.

Embodiment

Author Maria Harris talks about a freeing concept called "embodiment": a bodily activity that makes our spirits whole. For some, embodiment may come through music; for others, through cooking; for others, through writing, walking, etc.[5] When we are involved in an embodiment experience, we are often in such a state of intense creative concentration and ecstasy that we lose track of time and the needs of our egos as well. Theologian Dorothee Soelle says that at such moments "the divine self within us is set free."[6] The late conductor Leonard Bernstein observed:

> *At the end of such performances, performances which I call good, it takes minutes before I know where I am—in what hall, in what country—or who I am. Suddenly, I become aware that there is clapping, that I must bow. It's very difficult. But marvelous. A sort of ecstasy which is nothing more and nothing less than a loss of ego. You don't exist. It's exactly the same sort of ecstasy as the trance you are in when you are composing and you are inspired. You don't know what time it is or what's going by.*[7]

Where do you find your experiences of embodiment? How do these times of embodiment make you feel? Discuss.

Moonlighting

The following reflection is borrowed from journal-writing expert Kay Leigh Hagan. Try doing as she suggests.

> *Imagine that you have been invited to teach a class at a school for life experiences. Drawing from areas of passion, expertise, and skill in your own life, you may teach anything you want in any manner that you wish. "Roadtripping: Cross-Country Driving for Fun and Adventure," "Creating a Sacred Space in Your Home," and "Surprise Packages: Making Eggrolls, Dolmas, Tamales, and Other Wrapped Food" are in my own curriculum. Write the course description for the school catalog here.*[8]

F O O D A S S Y M B O L

Have each guest bring a food that he or she finds particularly creative. (This item can certainly be purchased from a store or bakery if physical or creative energies are at a minimum.) I find "hidden foods" intriguing, and I delight in breads and pastries stuffed with unexpected and exciting ingredients. The following are three of my favorite "hidden food" recipes.

HOLLY'S STUFFED PIZZA DELUXE
(VEGETARIAN MAIN DISH)

1 package of 2 ready-made pie crusts
4 eggs
1 15-ounce carton ricotta cheese
1 small onion, chopped
1 cup grated parmesan
1 tablespoon chopped parsley
Salt and pepper (to taste)
2 tablespoons olive oil
1/2 teaspoon dried oregano
2 cloves crushed garlic
1 8-ounce can tomato sauce
1 6-ounce can tomato paste
1 small can sliced or chopped black olives
1/2 pound thinly sliced mozzarella cheese
1 large green bell pepper or 1 large sweet red bell pepper

Place bottom crust in a 10-inch pie plate. Mix together eggs, ricotta, onion, parmesan, parsley, and salt and pepper to taste. Set aside. Heat the olive oil in a small saucepan and add the garlic and the oregano, stirring until the garlic begins to turn gold. Then add the tomato sauce, tomato paste, and black olives. Season with salt and pepper to taste. Seed the green or red pepper and slice into long, thin strips. Get out the mozzarella cheese.

Now you are ready to assemble: Spread half the ricotta mixture in the prepared pie shell. Arrange over this half of the mozzarella slices. Cover with half the tomato sauce and then put half the bell pepper slices on top. Repeat all the layers and then cover with the top pie crust and pinch the edges together. With a sharp knife make three long parallel slashes through the top crust. Bake the stuffed pizza in a 400-degree oven for about 35–40 minutes. Let stand for half an hour before serving. Serves 8.

For Stuffed Pizza Florentine: Cook 1 10-ounce package frozen spinach. Drain and press through a sieve. Substitute the spinach layer for the bell pepper layer when assembling.

STUFFED PARTY BREAD

1 loaf unsliced Vienna or Italian bread
3/4 pound grated Swiss cheese
8 ounces fresh mushrooms, chopped
3–4 scallions and stems, thinly sliced
2 tablespoons poppy seed or toasted sesame seed
1/2 teaspoon seasoned salt
1 cup butter
1 1/2 teaspoons lemon juice
1 tablespoon dry mustard

Score bread by slicing lengthwise to within 1/2 inch from bottom of
loaf in 1-inch sections. Turn and do the same thing in the other direction. Stuff all the little openings in the bread with cheese and mushrooms. Sprinkle onions, seeds, and seasoned salt over the top. Melt
butter and add lemon juice and dry mustard; stir together. Gently
spoon butter mixture over loaf. Wrap in foil. Bake at 350 degrees
for about 40 minutes. When serving, place a fork nearby. Guests
can serve themselves by pulling pieces off with a fork. Serves 9–12.
This is delicious as an appetizer or with a good, hearty pot of soup.

STUFFED SURPRISE LOAF

1 loaf round sourdough bread
1/3 cup Italian dressing or olive oil sprinkled with your favorite herbs
Your choice of the following or any other creative ingredients you can think of:
Shredded cheese (choose your favorite or a combination)
Thinly sliced cucumber
Thinly sliced lettuce of any kind or fresh spinach
Thinly sliced tomato
Chopped scallions or thinly sliced red onion
Sliced meat: salami, roast turkey, etc.

Cut slice from top of bread loaf. Take out the inside of the bread leaving 1/2 inch of shell all around. (Sprinkle some olive oil and herbs over this discarded bread, toast it in the oven, and use it as croutons later on.) Brush top and inside of shell with Italian dressing or herbed olive oil. Fill shell with layers of ingredients of your choice, beginning and ending with cheese. Put top back on. Wrap in foil. Bake 45 minutes at 350 degrees. Cool for a few minutes before cutting into wedges. Serve hot or cold. Makes 6 servings. If you choose to use cheese and no meat, this can be a delicious vegetarian entrée or appetizer.

THREE

BOAST, TOAST, AND BOAST SOME MORE

THEME

This feast celebrates self-esteem and feeling positive, healthy, and whole about who one is.

UNDERSTANDING THE NEED FOR SOME HEALTHY BOASTING

Not long ago I was invited to a women's ritual in which the guests did not know each other well. We sat in a circle around a fire, and the leader encouraged us to introduce ourselves by saying our whole names and then "I am a wonderful woman because . . ." This was strangely difficult! Women especially are experts at introducing themselves by telling all the things that they are not. I had to work on giving myself permission to introduce myself in this self-affirming way.

Most of us need to practice taking pride and joy in who we are and what we have experienced and achieved. Remember, "Love your neighbor *as yourself*." We can't do much neighbor-loving if our own self-esteem is pathetic and impoverished. A little public boasting in a supportive, safe, and hospitable environment can be a very good thing! Generating some private affirmations at home can be healing and helpful as well.

PLANNING AHEAD

Ask everyone to bring to the feast a symbol or object that represents his or her personal power.

REFLECTING TOGETHER: OPPORTUNITIES FOR DISCUSSION

(The leader selects those topics and activities that are most appropriate for the group and for which there is time.)

Boast, Toast, and Boast Some More
At three different times during the meal (perhaps after appetizers, soup, or salad; after main course; after dessert), get enthusiastically involved in some fine toasting as each person gets three rounds of unabashed and gleeful boasting. The group may want to show its appreciation at any point by clapping, stomping, hooting, singing, etc. Keep filling guests' goblets each time with wassail. (See "Food as Symbol.")

- *Round 1. Wonderful man or woman:*
  Each participant says, in turn, "I am [whole name]. I am a wonderful woman [or man] because . . ." The whole assembly then lifts a glass and says "Here's to [first name]!"
- *Round 2. Hardest hurdle:*
  Each participant says, in turn, "I am [first name]. The hardest hurdle I ever overcame was . . ." The whole assembly again lifts a glass and says "Here's to [first name]!"
- *Round 3. Best accomplishment:*
  Each participant says, in turn, "I am [first name]. The accomplishment I feel best about is . . ." The whole assembly again lifts a glass and says "Here's to [first name]!"

Ritualist Starhawk suggests that if someone finds it impossible to engage in such self-praise, encourage that person either to speak aloud or to write down the negative judgments that are blocking a positive response. These judgments can then be torn up or burned.[1]

Personal Power Symbols

Take time to listen to all the participants share why they chose their particular symbols to bring and what meanings these symbols hold for them.

Prayers of Thanksgiving for Ourselves

Hand out pieces of paper and ask each guest to write a prayer of thanksgiving, thanking God for himself or herself. Encourage persons to give themselves permission to do this with forthrightness and delight. After about fifteen minutes (or more time if needed) gather in a circle. Invite those who wish to share their prayers aloud to do so. After each prayer is offered, the group responds: "We thank you God for [first name]." This creates a sacred conclusion to this time of toasting and boasting, which may be followed by a song of praise and thanksgiving.

SETTING THE TABLE

Goblets are fundamental to this feast with all its toasting. The more grandiose the goblets, the better.

FOOD AS SYMBOL

One festive drink to share at this feast would be wassail, an old Anglo-Saxon drink whose name means "wholeness." I make all kinds of wassail, depending on what ingredients I have on hand. All my variations start out with apple juice or apple cider, which I then combine with orange juice, cranberry juice, apricot nectar, or pineapple juice.

You can make this delicious concoction either in a big pot on the stove or in a percolator. If you want to use a percolator, put cinnamon sticks, whole cloves, whole allspice, and some brown sugar in the percolator basket and perk like coffee. If using a pot, stir in the brown sugar and then use powdered or strained versions of the spices. Experiment and discover what variation of ingredients is your favorite.

This mirthful feast can be prepared by the hosting individual or family, or guests can be asked to bring food for a potluck.

Four

THEME

This potluck feast lifts up the newness of each stage of life as it focuses on the recognition of one's strengths and opportunities at every age. This feast would be appropriate for a birthday celebration, a retirement party, a new job, or a geographical move (i.e., any occasion that calls for the celebration of new beginnings.)

PLANNING AHEAD

Ask guests to bring to this feast a symbol of something they are birthing or bringing into existence at this particular stage of their lives. Ask them also to bring a food to share which represents their "changing tastes." (See "Food as Symbol.")

REFLECTING TOGETHER: OPPORTUNITIES FOR DISCUSSION

(The leader selects those topics and activities that are most appropriate for the group and for which there is time.)

New Birth

What new birth are you experiencing at this stage of your life? Take time to reflect together on the symbols that everyone has brought. What support do you continue to need in this birthing process?

Turning Points and Opportunities

Have each person draw a vertical line down the center of a piece of paper. On one side, write "Turning Point." On the other side, write "Opportunity." What turning points and opportunities do you find yourself experiencing right now? After a few minutes, share what's comfortable.

Coming into One's Own

In her book *At Seventy: A Journal,* author May Sarton writes:

> *At Hartford College in Connecticut I had been asked to talk about old*
> *age. . . . In the course of it I said, "This is the best time of my life. I*
> *love being old." At that point a voice from the audience asked loudly,*
> *"Why is it good to be old?" I answered spontaneously . . . , "Because I*
> *am more myself than I have ever been. There is less conflict. I am hap-*
> *pier, more balanced, and" (I heard myself say rather aggressively)*
> *"more powerful." I felt it was rather an odd word "powerful," but I*
> *think it is true. It might have been more accurate to say "I am better*
> *able to use my powers." I am surer of what my life is all about.*[1]

When asked why it is good to be old, May Sarton replies, "Because I am more myself than I have ever been." What does she mean by this? Could you say this of your own life right now? Why or why not? What are the gifts of your present stage of life that you have not experienced before? Talk together.

The Capacity to Act

I like to define power simply as "the capacity to act." If power is the capacity to act, in what ways are you powerful? Where is your power? Where is your powerlessness? Where does your powerlessness come from: yourself, society, others? What blocks are preventing you from claiming your power? How can you start disassembling these blocks? Discuss.

Some Questions about Your Present Stage of Life
Ask yourself:

What do you want for yourself?
What does God want for you?
What are you no longer willing to keep silent about?
How are you loving yourself and treating yourself gently these days?

Share your ideas.

Art as Meditation
The following exercise is inspired by St. Ignatius of Loyola (1495–1556). [2] Imagine that you are looking back on your entire life from the perspective of one at the end of life. As you imagine yourself at age ninety or one hundred reviewing the stage of life where you are now, what do you see? How does this stage fit into the picture of your entire existence? With a pencil, crayons, or markers, try to draw or chart where you are now in relation to your whole life. Use colors, words, images. After you're finished, spend some time talking with others.

Changing Tastes
If there is time, talk for a few minutes about the foods brought and why they represent each person's changing tastes. (See "Food as Symbol.")

SETTING THE TABLE

An appropriate focal point for this feast would be a big bowl of eggs, fresh from the farm or grocery. If you wish, you may hardboil them and color them. For a thought-provoking centerpiece on your table, place everyone's symbols of new birth around the bowl of eggs.

FOOD AS SYMBOL

Throughout our lives, we cultivate new tastes for different cuisines and often expand our culinary repertoire by suddenly liking Vietnamese food, vegetarian fare, etc. Ask the guests to bring to this feast foods that represent to them their changing tastes. This further emphasizes the ever-changing and ever-transforming pattern of our lives.

FIVE

FLAMBOYANT FANTASY: AN OUTRAGEOUS FEAST

THEME

This feast encourages the outrageous in all of us, that outrageousness which permits us to get in touch with our most honest, committed, and flamboyant selves.[1]

PLANNING AHEAD

Ask guests to bring an outrageous food that speaks of excess: the creamiest cheesecake, the fudgiest sundae, the pizza with the most toppings. (See "Food as Symbol.")

REFLECTING TOGETHER: OPPORTUNITIES FOR DISCUSSION

(The leader selects topics and activities that are most appropriate for the group and for which there is time.)

Outrageousness

Think about the smaller words found in the word *outrageous: rage* and *outrage.* What in your life causes you rage? What elements of society make you outraged? How can you better get in touch with these sources of rage and outrage? How can you help yourself to handle your rage constructively? Where is your support? In what ways can you and others change the world to bring about justice?

Name two outrageous things you have done in your life. How did these outrageous acts make you feel? What were the consequences? Would you like to do these things again?

Outrageousness is about having courage and being willing to buck the system. In what ways does the world need you to be outrageous right now? Talk together.

Who are the most outrageous people you know? How have they inspired you to be courageous, to take risks in your own life? Share.

In her book *Outrageous Acts and Everyday Rebellions,* Gloria Steinem says:

> *I now often end lectures with an organizer's deal. If each person in the room promises that in the twenty-four hours beginning the very next day she or he will do at least* one outrageous thing *in the cause of simple justice, then I promise I will, too. It doesn't matter whether the act is as small as saying, "Pick it up yourself" . . . or as large as calling a strike. . . . The world one day later won't be quite the same. . . . We will have such a good time that we will never again get up in the morning saying, "Will I do anything outrageous?" but only "What outrageous act will I do today?"*[2]

What outrageous acts, large or small, might be on your agenda this week? Talk with one another.

The Outlaw

In *Life Maps,* authors James Fowler and Sam Keen talk about the part in each of us that is "The Outlaw." The Outlaw:

- Wants to discover the depths of the self that lie beneath all the roles and obligations.
- Wants to explore the uncontrolled forces that have been held in check.
- Begins to question all the former values.[3]

Is there a keenly felt Outlaw in you that wants to break away? What is your Outlaw encouraging you to do right now?

Forbidden Five

This gem is from writer Julia Cameron:

> List five things you are not allowed to do: kill your boss, scream in church, go outside naked, make a scene, quit your job. Now do that thing on paper. Write it, draw it, paint it, act it out, collage it. Now put some music on and dance it.[4]

Flamboyant Fantasy

What fun it is to cook up an outrageous and flamboyant fantasy! Making up fantasies and imagining outrageous acts can stretch us and allow us within a safe environment to look at acts of daring, possible consequences, and what we would really like to do if we were allowed. Fantasies can help us determine how we might incorporate a few of our dreams into our everyday existence.

If you could create a fantasy of self-indulgence and personal power, what would it be? Write it down, and don't let any voices of judgment come near. What did that feel like to write that fantasy? What did you learn about yourself? Share with one another what's comfortable.

CREATING THE ENVIRONMENT

Wear outrageous clothes. Try a costume party. Decorate the dining area in any outrageous theme you please.

FOOD AS SYMBOL

Outrageous food is called for here—the food you have longed for, the food you were never allowed to eat enough of. Now is the time to indulge! Have everyone bring an outrageous food that speaks of excess: the creamiest cheesecake, the fudgiest sundae, the pizza with the most toppings. My relatives tell me that my goal in life is to cram the most calories per square inch humanly possible into a small piece of dessert. The following excessive, knock 'em dead recipe is true to form.

OUTRAGEOUS BROWNIES

1 box of brownie mix for 13 x 9-inch pan (or your favorite
from-scratch recipe)
Enough chocolate candy bars to layer side by side in 13" by 9" pan
(Flat candy bars are best: my favorites are Hershey bars—
Milk Chocolate or Cookies 'n Mint—or Nestle's Crunch bars)

Grease 13 x 9-inch pan. Pour half of brownie batter in pan. Layer
with all the candy bars. Pour other half of batter on top. Bake as
directed in brownie recipe. Cut into small pieces lest guests expire at
table. (They would die happy, though.)

Also consider trying the outrageous "Chocolate Cheesecake Heart in Cookie Crust"
found in chapter 18, "Hearts!"

Six

BROADENING THE BOUNDARIES: A GLOBAL POTLUCK

THEME

This international feast examines the ancient concept of hospitality as it explores what significance hospitality can have for us today.

PLANNING AHEAD

In planning for this international potluck, ask guests to attach little cards to their dishes explaining what kind of food it is and in what country it has its origins.

UNDERSTANDING HOSPITALITY

The word *hospitality* is from the Greek *hospes*, which means a host or a guest. Webster's defines *hospitality* as "the act, practice, or quality of receiving and entertaining strangers or guests in a friendly and generous way."

Hospitality as Holy Duty[1]
Henri Nouwen writes:

> *If there is any concept worth restoring to its evocative potential, it is the concept of hospitality. It is one of the richest biblical terms that can deepen and broaden our insight in our relationship to our fellow human beings.*

Old and New Testament stories not only show how serious our obligation is to welcome the stranger in our home, but they also tell us that guests are carrying precious gifts with them, which they are eager to reveal to a receptive host.[2]

In biblical times, hospitality was regarded as a law, a holy duty. First Peter 4:9 says, "Be hospitable to one another without complaining." Romans 12:13 says, "Contribute to the needs of the saints; practice hospitality" (RSV). In James 2:14–17 is found perhaps the strongest of all the admonitions to hospitality:

> *What good is it, my brothers and sisters, if you say you have faith but do not have works? Can faith save you? If a brother or sister is naked and lacks daily food, and one of you says to them, "Go in peace; keep warm and eat your fill," and yet you do not supply their bodily needs, what is the good of that? So faith by itself, if it has no works, is dead.*

A Modern Story of Middle Eastern Hospitality

Vince Kavaloski, who serves as cochair of the Wisconsin Ecumenical Partnership for Peace and Justice, writes:

> *I recall vividly our own numerous experiences of warmth and hospitality . . . when Jane and I led a Wisconsin Interfaith delegation to the Middle East. In Nazareth a group of us went into an Arab bakery for coffee and rolls and talked with the proprietor, Amad, about his family, the "Intifada." . . . One topic led to another in the languorous heat of the Galilean afternoon. Finally, as we rose to leave, Amad thanked us for visiting and then refused our payment. Among the Arab people, he explained, when people open their hearts to one another, they are*

no longer stranger but guests, and guests are to be given hospitality.
"Hospitality is holy," Amad said, "and cannot be bought."[3]

REFLECTING TOGETHER: OPPORTUNITIES FOR DISCUSSION

(The leader selects those topics and activities that are most appropriate for the group and for which there is time.)

Definitions of Hospitality

Joetta Handrich Schlabach, in the world cookbook *Extending the Table,*" writes, "A simple beverage and an attentive ear will honor a stranger and a friend."[4] Think about this quotation and its definition of hospitality. When did you receive such hospitality? How did it make you feel?

A Haitian proverb says: *"Manje kwit pa gen met."* ("Cooked food has no owner.") This definition of hospitality is expansive. Would you like to broaden your circle of companions at mealtime? How might this be done? Talk together.

The following four Bible stories deal with the subject of hospitality:

1. Elijah and the widow of Zarephath (1 Kings 17:8–16)
2. Jesus and Zacchaeus (Luke 19:1–10)
3. Jesus on the road to Emmaus (Luke 24:13–35)
4. Paul and Lydia (Acts 16:13–15)

What does each of these stories have to say about hospitality? What does each story inspire you to do in your own life? Read all these stories together, or have four persons or four small groups each select one scripture and report back to the larger group.

Hospitality and Community

Today we live in a rushed and demanding world in which there is little dropping in or dropping by, let alone much sharing of pooled resources or intentional community-building time. Henri Nouwen writes:

> *In our world full of strangers, estranged from their own past, culture, and country, from their neighbors, friends and family, from their deepest self and their God, we witness a painful search for a hospitable place where life can be lived without fear and where community can be found.*[5]

Where is your community that nurtures and supports you? Are you spending enough time with these particular people? Share your thoughts.

Hospitality and God

God is our Divine Host or Hostess who is the creating spirit of the universe. Discuss how God has provided hospitality to you in your life.

Read Psalm 136. Try writing your own Psalm of Thanksgiving for the ways God has been hospitable and welcoming to you. If you like, share what you have written.

How are you being hospitable to God? Do you welcome God into your life? Discuss how you are cultivating that relationship.

Part of being hospitable to God involves receiving with grace the gifts that God, the Welcoming One, is trying to give us. Read Matthew 7:7–11. Is God trying to give you a gift right now that you are not able to accept? If so, why might it be? Talk together.

Holding the World in God's Light: A Guided Imagery Prayer[6]

When you see the earth from the moon, you don't see any divisions there of nations or states. This might be the symbol, really, for the new mythology to come. That is the country that we are going to be celebrating. And those are the people that we are one with.[7]

At the beginning of this time of reflection, go around the room and ask each person to share briefly how he or she has been affected by the world news during this past week.

Pass out "earth marbles." (Many nature stores or scientific-supply shops sell green or blue translucent or iridescent marbles for a reasonable price.) Remind persons that the marbles that they will hold in their hands during the following prayer time represent our planet.

The leader should read the following very slowly so as to provide ample time for reflection between phrases:

Leader: We are going to be spending a few minutes in a prayer of guided meditation. Get comfortable. Take anything heavy off your lap. Close your eyes. Take a couple of slow, deep breaths . . . in and out. Feel yourself holding the planet in your hand.

Imagine the earth surrounded by the Healing Light of God. . . . See our planet radiant and glowing in God's Light. . . .

As you think about the whole earth, picture in your mind your own community. Where are the divisions? Where is the fear? Where is the tension? . . . Imagine your own community bathed in God's love.

Again, picture the globe. Move in your mind to the east. Move to a part of the world east of you which particularly needs healing. Imagine those people held in God's Light. Picture the people there comforted and at peace.

Taking all the time you need, move slowly around the world, stopping from place to place. Remain with whatever people need help and hold them in the Light of God. Travel in your mind around the world. . . .

(Long pause—at least two minutes.)

Leader: Imagine your hands and feet becoming the hands and feet of God. Picture yourself carrying the Spirit of God out into your community and throughout the world. How might this happen?

When you are ready, open your eyes and come back into this place and this room.

Encourage persons to take their earth marbles home and put them in a place where they are likely to come across them each day. They will thus be reminded of the need for hospitality, prayer, and advocacy for sisters and brothers around the world.

CREATING THE ENVIRONMENT

At the beginning of this feast, set up a picture or poster of the earth as viewed from space, or put a globe on a prominent table. Play music from around the world. Invite a dancing or singing group from another country to perform. Hang maps of different countries all over the dining area. Other possible wall decorations might include ethnic pictures, symbols, rugs, towels, or pieces of fabric. Tablecloths may also be made from imported fabric pieces (if not too valuable and able to withstand spills).

A dress-up feast may well be in order. Have participants dress in the ethnic costume of their foremothers and forefathers or in the dress of a country with which they feel a special affinity.

FOOD AS SYMBOL

This is an international potluck. Ask everyone to bring a little card with his or her dish, explaining what kind of food it is and in what country it has its origins.

Some of my favorite international cookbooks are:

Extending the Table, by Joetta Handrich Schlabach
More-with-Less Cookbook, by Doris Janzen Longacre
Sundays at the Moosewood Restaurant, by Mollie Katzen
Betty Crocker's International Cookbook
The Vegetarian Epicure, Book Two, by Anna Thomas

One of our family's favorite international dishes is Thai Chicken Satay. We love this tasty recipe for summer grilling.

THAI CHICKEN SATAY

Marinade:
1 tablespoon ground coriander or 1/4 cup fresh, chopped coriander
(also called cilantro)
6 cloves crushed garlic
1 teaspoon salt
1 finely chopped onion
2 tablespoons brown sugar
Juice of 2 limes
2 tablespoons vegetable oil
2 tablespoons soy sauce

Meat:
6 whole chicken breasts, boned, skinned, cut into cubes

Combine marinade ingredients and marinate chicken overnight or at least a couple of hours. Put chicken on skewers. Grill about 10 minutes until browned.

Peanut sauce:
2 cloves garlic, minced
1 tablespoon vegetable or peanut oil
1 1/2 cups water
1/2–1 teaspoon red hot pepper flakes (to taste)
1/2 teaspoon salt
2 tablespoons sugar
1 cup peanut butter, smooth or crunchy

Fry garlic in oil for 1 minute. Add everything else except peanut butter. When the mixture starts to simmer, add the peanut butter and stir well. If it's too thick for your liking, add some more water. Simmer for 5 more minutes, stirring often.

Serve grilled chicken with peanut sauce. Serve with rice or rice noodles. Makes 6 servings.

CHICKEN LO MEIN

2 cups fresh bean sprouts
8–16 ounces cooked chicken (depending how meaty you like it)
1 1/2 cups grated carrots (about 2 carrots)
3 cups snow peas
1 cup finely chopped cabbage or bok choy (optional)
1 pound thin spaghetti
9 tablespoons soy sauce (divided)
7 tablespoons peanut oil (divided)
6 teaspoons sesame oil (divided)
1 1/2 tablespoons minced ginger root
2 teaspoons crushed garlic
2 onions, finely chopped

Boil large pot of water. Add thin spaghetti and cook, following directions on package. Cut chicken into strips or small cubes. Remove stems and strings from snow peas and cut into narrow slivers. Place large skillet or wok on high heat. Add 7 tablespoons soy sauce, 5 tablespoons peanut oil, 4 teaspoons sesame oil, 4 teaspoons dry sherry, ginger root, garlic, and onion. Heat until boiling and cook for 1 minute, stirring constantly. Mix in the chicken and the rest of the vegetables. Cook for 2–3 minutes, stirring, and then set skillet or wok aside. Drain pasta and put back in the cooking pot. Toss the drained pasta with 2 tablespoons soy sauce, 2 tablespoons peanut oil, and 2 teaspoons sesame oil. Add to chicken and vegetable mixture in skillet or wok. Stir all ingredients together over medium high heat for several minutes or until sufficiently hot to serve. Makes 8 servings.

SEVEN

THEME

This feast takes a look at nurture and comfort as it challenges us to ask: How is it that we take care of ourselves?

PLANNING AHEAD

Invite each person to bring a place setting, along with any other objects, symbols, or decorations that represent him or her and which then will become a personal altar.[1] For this potluck feast, encourage guests to bring any food that comforts or delights them.

UNDERSTANDING THE NEED FOR COMFORT

As a friend departs, we often hear, "Goodbye. Take care." But do we take care? Do most of us have any clue as to how to be gentle to ourselves? When I feel physically exhausted and emotionally empty, I am trying more and more these days to stop and ask deliberately, "What do I need to help me better care for myself right now?"[2] Taking the time to ask myself this question provides considerable insight. After I stop to reflect, I find I feel less anxiety and discomfort and usually can discover precisely what my primary need is. Sometimes it's food; sometimes it's companionship; sometimes it's sleep. By asking this question intentionally, it is easier to name the need exactly rather than trying to substitute one need for another. When I'm exhausted, for example, sleep is what I need rather than the food I often turn to.

51

REFLECTING TOGETHER: OPPORTUNITIES FOR DISCUSSION

(The leader selects those topics and activities that are most appropriate for the group and for which there is time.)

Simple Pleasures

In *Prayers to the Moon,* author Kay Leigh Hagan suggests the following self-discovery exercise, beginning with asking yourself, "What brings you pleasure? Make a list of 'simple pleasures,' those small things that delight and surprise you, cause you to pause and enjoy the moment: a peaking blossom, a cloud splashed by the setting sun, a letter from a friend, unexpected praise or recognition."[3]

What are the simple pleasures that bring you delight? How might you go about naming them and offering yourself the opportunity to experience them more often? Talk together.

Basking

What do you think of when you hear the word *basking?* Kay Leigh Hagan writes, "Butterflies run on solar power. Cells in the design of their wings collect the warmth that powers their flight. When you see a butterfly at rest, perched on a flower, spreading its wings, it is said to be 'basking,' pausing to gather energy for future movement."[4] What are some examples of basking in your life? Do you give yourself permission to bask as often as you would wish?

Personal Altars

Take time during the meal to observe one another's place settings and to talk about why certain guests brought certain items.

Food of Comfort and Delight

Go around the table and share why guests chose particular foods to prepare and what memories they associate with them.

Examining Self-Nurture

How do you nurture yourself? What people, places, things, and activities do you associate with joy and comfort? Divide a piece of paper into three columns, headed "Nurturing People," "Nurturing Places/Things," and "Nurturing Activities."[5] As you compile your lists, does anything surprise you? Are you spending too much of your leisure time in nonnurturing activities? What might you like to change? Share your ideas.

Affirmations of Self-Care

When all participants have had sufficient time to reflect on at least one of the previous exercises, go around the circle three times, asking them to affirm what they are currently doing or will do to care for themselves. (Anyone is free to pass.) For example:

I give myself permission to read the magazines I love.
I will purchase a season ticket to the theater series I enjoy.
I will continue to have lunch with a friend once a week.

End this time of individual affirmation by saying together:

I value myself. (repeat)
I am precious in God's sight. (repeat)
I will take care. (repeat)

ART AS MEDITATION

You may make bath salts ahead of time and distribute them as a pleasant party favor, or the group may wish to stir up a batch together. This recipe may be doubled or tripled depending on the number of guests.

COMFORTING BATH SALTS

6 cups Epsom salt (available in drugstores)
2 tablespoon glycerin (available in drugstores)
A few drops of food coloring of your favorite color
(or you could make batches of several colors)
Women's perfume or men's cologne (experiment to see how strong you like it)

Mix together. Put in little bags or jars for guests to take home. A scallop shell makes a pretty scoop. Use about 1/4-1/2 cup per bath and pour in tub under hot running water. Enjoy a sensuous and comforting bath!

In the last batch I made, I mixed 1/2 teaspoon of oil of peppermint with the Epsom salts and glycerin and colored the salts pink. Eucalyptus oil is also one of my favorite vivifying scents to use in these salts.

Another "Art as Meditation" possibility for the feast of comfort is "Summer Garden Bath Oil," found in chapter 14, "Nature's Bounty: A Summer Picnic."

SETTING THE TABLE

Set the table with the place settings and symbols that each person has brought from home.

FOOD AS SYMBOL

Invite guests to bring to this feast any food that comforts or delights them. Don't worry about the variety; if a meal turns out to be all appetizers or all desserts, so be it.

EIGHT

THEME

This feast commemorates the creative and feminine power of God, called "Wisdom," or in Greek Sophia, as it reveres the wisdom that is found and passed on through each one of us.

PLANNING AHEAD

Depending on the number of guests and the size of the recipe of Wisdom Croissants (see "Food as Symbol"), each person is asked to bring two or three personal proverbs or "rules to live by," which have been typed or written with a pen on thin strips of paper. These will be inserted and baked into the Wisdom Croissants to be prepared at the feast. This feast is a potluck; ask guests to bring a dish taught to them by a mentor, a teacher, or a wise loved one.

REFLECTING TOGETHER: OPPORTUNITIES FOR DISCUSSION

(The leader selects those topics and activities that are most appropriate for the group and for which there is time.)

The Host or Hostess's Welcome and Offering of Praise to God's Wisdom

The following prayer of thanksgiving from the book *Wisdom's Feast*,[1] adapted from Ecclesiasticus 24, may be used as a welcome or as a table blessing.

*Wisdom, you came forth from the Most High, as a mist you cov-
ered the earth.*

*You were in the pillar of cloud; you led our forebears out of slav-
ery into freedom.*

*You are like a mighty oak; you stretch forth your branches—
branches of glory and grace.*

You are like a vine, filled with flowers that yield fruits of glory.

*Wisdom calls: "Come unto me, you that desire me, and be filled
with good things."*

*For all that eat shall still hunger for you; all that drink shall still
thirst for you.*

*You are like a life-giving stream; you water the gardens you have
planted.*

*Let us come enjoy Wisdom's bounty; let us rejoice in her goodness;
let us find life in abundance. Amen.*

Wisdom Sayings

Take time during the meal to enjoy the Wisdom Croissants and to talk about everyone's personal proverbs or "rules to live by."

A Three-Part Toast to Wisdom

As in the "Boast, Toast, and Boast Some More" feast (see chapter 3), participants are encouraged to offer a toast at three different times during the meal (perhaps after appetizers or salad;
after main course; after dessert).

∾ Round 1. To Wisdom:

One person says these words adapted from Colossians 1:

You exist before all things, and you hold all things together.
In you all things were created, everything visible and everything
invisible.
You are the image of the unseen God, the first born of all creation.
All fullness is found in you, everything in heaven, and everything
on earth.[2]

The whole assembly then lifts a glass and says, "Here's to Wisdom!"

∾ *Round 2. To a wise one:*

Each person proposes a toast to a wise one who has been a role model or mentor. Each person at the table is encouraged to share his or her mentor's name and the wisdom that he or she imparted. The whole assembly lifts a glass as each person shares and responds by saying: "Here's to [mentor's name]!"

∾ *Round 3 : To each of us:*

Each person names him or herself and some wisdom that he or she is sharing: "I am [first name] and the wisdom that I am passing on to others is . . ." The whole assembly lifts a glass each time around and responds by saying: "Here's to [first name]!"

Art as Meditation

(Hand out blank white paper and a variety of markers, crayons, or colored pencils—whatever art supplies you have at hand.)

In a recent magazine article, writer Roger Rosenblatt says, "Children are born hunting for directions. . . . Parents are meant to give direction. Parents are maps."[3] Think of yourself as a wise teacher who is passing along what you have learned to another. Draw the map of life that you would pass on to a son, daughter, friend, or protégé. Show the obstacles (blocks, hindrances) and the helpers (guides, resources, assistance) you believe exist.[4] Use colors, pictures, images, and words. After about half an hour, gather back together and discuss your maps with one another, sharing only what is comfortable.

Conclusion of Feast: Circle Dance

Ask all participants to gather in a circle, hold hands, and dance to "We Are Dancing Wisdom's Circle." (This song, adapted from Carole Etzler Eagleheart, is sung to the melody of the folk hymn "Jacob's Ladder.") Sing through twice.

> *We are dancing Wisdom's circle,*
> *We are dancing Wisdom's circle,*
> *We are dancing Wisdom's circle,*
> *Sisters, [brothers,] all! (if only women, sing: "Sisters one and all!")*[5]

Final Blessing and Commission

Continue holding hands in a circle and repeat line by line after leader:

> May Wisdom be in our minds, and in our thinking (repeat);
> May Wisdom be in our hearts and in our perceiving (repeat);
> May Wisdom be in our mouths and in our speaking (repeat);
> May Wisdom be in our hands and in our working (repeat);
> May Wisdom be in our feet and in our walking (repeat);
> May Wisdom be in our bodies and in our loving (repeat).
> May we go with Wisdom! (repeat)

> *Leader:* Amen![6]

FOOD AS SYMBOL

Guests are asked to bring a dish taught to them by a mentor or teacher or wise loved one.

Wisdom Croissants

At the time of the feast, the host or hostess collects all the wisdom sayings composed by the guests and bakes them into croissants. These may be homemade croissants or purchased in a can, ready to bake. Serve the croissants at dinner and discuss the sayings (see "Reflecting Together").

NINE

THEME

This feast invites us into a state of wonder through stimulation and awareness received through our five senses.

PLANNING AHEAD AND CREATING THE ENVIRONMENT

Encourage guests to dress sensually and wear costumes or clothes that bring them delight. You may also invite them to bring along an object that awakens and arouses one of the five senses: sight, smell, hearing, taste, touch.

SETTING THE TABLE

The feast of wonder calls for an especially pleasing centerpiece on the table or tables where the feast is to be celebrated. The host, hostess, or various guests may want to assemble a centerpiece of fresh fruit, flowers, vegetables, pine cones, etc. Or the sensory objects that the guests have brought may be arranged on a mirror or among lighted candles.

REFLECTING TOGETHER: OPPORTUNITIES FOR DISCUSSION

(The leader selects those topics and activities that are most appropriate for the group and for which there is time.)

Invocation for the Feast

Recite an appropriate gathering sentence, such as that from Psalm 34: "O taste and see that God is good!"[1]

Mindfulness

Thich Nhat Hanh and other Zen practitioners encourage a constant state of "mindfulness." Mindfulness teaches us to be fully aware of each experience, letting nothing remain unnoticed, taking nothing for granted. It is a way to live attentively and without regret. A well-known stanza of a poem by E. E. Cummings expresses the sentiments of thanksgiving and attentiveness which unite in the state of mindfulness:

> *i thank you God for most this amazing*
> *day: for the leaping greenly spirits of trees*
> *and a blue true dream of sky; and for everything*
> *which is natural which is infinite which is yes* [2]

Sit with those gathered for five minutes in silence and mindfulness. Smell the smells. See the sights. Hear the hushed sounds of the clocks ticking or the appliances humming. Appreciate the people gathered.

Everyday Sensual Pleasures

What in your everyday existence brings you sensual pleasure? (This might be kneading bread, taking a hot shower, playing in the garden, etc.) Are there any practices you might initiate which could bring you an increased sense of appreciation and wonder? Share your ideas.

A Voluptuous God

Thirteenth-century mystic Meister Eckhart has written, "God is voluptuous and delicious."[3] Have you ever experienced God in this way?

Capacity for Delight

Writer Julia Cameron talks about developing a "capacity for delight." In *The Artist's Way*, she reminisces about her beloved grandmother, who survived sixty-two years of marriage to an alcoholic gambler only by developing a capacity for delight in the small things of life. Cameron writes:

> *My grandmother was gone before I learned the lesson her letters were teaching: survival lies in sanity, and sanity lies in paying attention. Yes, her letters said, Dad's cough is getting worse, we have lost the house, there is no money and no work, but the tiger lilies are blooming, the lizard has found that spot of sun, the roses are holding despite the heat.*

Cameron goes on to say, "The quality of life is in proportion, always, to the capacity for delight. The capacity for delight is the gift of paying attention."[4]

What is your capacity for delight? What are those small things in life which you notice and which bring you joy? Talk together.

Appreciating Your Five Senses: Guided Imagery[5]
The leader should read the following very slowly so as to provide ample time for reflection between phrases.

Leader: Close your eyes. Sit quietly and relax. Get rid of any tension you feel. Take a couple of slow, deep breaths . . . in and out, in and out.

Feel your eyes sitting there behind your eyelids and think about all the sights your eyes have enabled you to see. Consider your eyes and how your sense of sight has enhanced your life. Thank God for being able to see.

Now think about your nose and your sense of smell. Reflect on the aromas you have smelled during your life—both good and bad—and all that your nose has taught you. Thank God for your sense of smell.

Feel your ears resting on either side of your head. Recall the various sounds you have heard in your life and what these sounds have meant to you. Reflect on the variety of all these sounds. Appreciate your hearing and thank God for being able to hear.

Now think about your sense of taste and feel your tongue as it sits in your mouth and touches your teeth. What have been some of your favorite tastes throughout your life? Has your sense of taste ever warned you of something that was harmful to eat? Thank God for being able to taste.

Feel your skin all over your body and reflect on your sense of touch. Think about your clothes as they are touching your skin right now. Think about everything you are experiencing right at this moment through your sense of touch. Reflect on the many different kinds of touch you have experienced during your life. Thank God that your sense of touch is helping you to receive information.

Sit quietly in a state of awareness as you appreciate everything that comes through your five senses.

When you are ready, slowly open your eyes and focus your attention back into this time and this place.

Take a few minutes to discuss anything that may have come to mind during the guided imagery.

Feast of the Five Senses

Flora Slosson Wuellner, author of *Prayer and Our Bodies*, says:

> *One of the holiest experiences I ever had was also one of the most bodily. My husband and I were invited to join a Jewish couple for their Sabbath meal. The food was simple, lovingly prepared, and flavorful. Between courses, we celebrated one of the five senses. At one point, our hosts passed around a flower for us to contemplate, touch, and smell. At another point, a piece of fruit was passed from hand to hand, with each person experiencing the fruit. Later, we sang a short song, delighting in the melody and in each other's voices. This sensory awareness of God's gifts was woven into the act of eating.*[6]

Plan the feast of wonder so that one of the five senses is celebrated between each course. Use the items that the guests have brought. Pass them around and savor them. As in the description above, singing may be one delightful way to celebrate the auditory sense.

ART AS MEDITATION

As a reminder to live in a state of mindfulness and appreciation, guests may want to make together and take home a little bag or jar of Balsam Potpourri. The recipe may be doubled or tripled depending on number of guests.

BALSAM POTPOURRI

2 cups dried balsam needles
1 cup dried lavender
2 cups dried rose petals
1 cup dried orange peel
2 teaspoons whole cloves
2 sticks cinnamon bark
2 teaspoons whole allspice
2 tablespoons orrisroot

Mix together. Add 8 drops of balsam oil (or however many drops smell right to you). Mix again. Fill plastic baggies and tie each with a ribbon.

Other "Art as Meditation" possibilities for the feast of wonder are Flower Potpourri and Summer Garden Bath Oil, found in chapter 14, "Nature's Bounty: A Summer Picnic," and the Comforting Bath Salts found in chapter 7, "Taking Care: A Feast of Comfort."

F O O D   A S   S Y M B O L

This feast may be prepared by one person or may be a potluck. Food should be presented in a particularly appetizing, lovely, and sensuous manner. Consider some hearty, aromatic Pasta Primavera with fresh garden herbs and vegetables, some rich dark chocolate mousse, or some steaming hot blueberry cobbler with vanilla ice cream. Think about your favorite recipes and choose ones that you enjoy preparing and that stimulate your senses.

One of my favorite gorgeous-looking and gorgeous-smelling recipes is Italian Minestrone, made with handfuls of hearty vegetables. This satisfying soup creates a taste sensation during any season. I am amazed that my teenaged son, who usually lives on cheeseburgers, requests this soup all the time. This recipe makes a big pot and is almost more like a stew than a soup.

ITALIAN MINESTRONE

6 tablespoons olive oil
2 cups chopped onion
4 teaspoons minced garlic
2 cups chopped carrots
2 cups chopped celery
2 cups chopped zucchini
1 cup chopped sweet red bell pepper
2 cups chopped green beans
4 teaspoons dried basil
1 teaspoon dried oregano
1 46-ounce can vegetable juice
4 cups chicken broth
1 28-ounce can tomatoes, chopped, with juice
1 15-ounce can dark red kidney beans, drained
1 15-ounce can light red kidney beans, drained
(Or for variety, you can use other beans, like garbanzos or black beans)
7 ounces dried pasta (shells, elbows, or whatever you like)
3 tablespoons minced fresh parsley or 2 tablespoons dried parsley flakes
Salt and pepper (to taste)
Chunk of parmesan cheese

Fry onion, garlic, carrots, and celery in olive oil over a moderate
heat for 5 minutes. Add zucchini, green pepper, green beans, basil,
and oregano and cook for 5 more minutes. Add vegetable juice,

chicken broth, tomatoes, and beans. Simmer for 10 minutes more. Add the pasta and parsley. Cook for another 10 minutes or until pasta is tender. Season with salt and pepper. Pass parmesan cheese and a grater around the table. Serves 12. Serve with "Stuffed Party Bread" (found in chapter 2, "Table of Creativity") and a green salad.

Note: An excellent resource for planning this feast is Diane Ackerman's book *A Natural History of the Senses.* Excerpts from various chapters may be selected, read aloud, and talked about throughout the course of the feast.

TEN

THEME

This feast gathers the members of a chosen family (relatives and/or friends) to celebrate love, friendship, community, and home.

UNDERSTANDING THE CHOSEN FAMILY

The constellation of the family is always changing. Many factors go into the formation of new families. Deaths occur; geographical moves bring changes. Some persons get along famously with their families of origin and intentionally seek out the friendship of brothers, sisters, mothers, fathers. Other persons do not get along well with their relatives and seek support from intimate friends who become a new family for them. This celebration for a chosen family provides participants with an opportunity to examine their own definitions of home and family. This feast would be appropriate for any occasion (such as birthday, retirement, or extraordinary achievement celebration) on which the host or hostess wishes to gather his or her chosen family in order to thank loved ones for their constancy and support.

PLANNING AHEAD

Ask guests to bring a food that especially represents home to them, and well as something for the table (a cup, dish, plate, bowl, etc.) that also symbolizes home.

REFLECTING TOGETHER: OPPORTUNITIES FOR DISCUSSION

(The leader selects those topics and activities that are most appropriate for the group and for which there is time.)

Introductory Welcome

In this welcome, the person hosting the feast shares the reason for this festive occasion and why the guests represent his or her chosen family. It is a time for the host or hostess to express gratitude and thanksgiving for circumstances of bonding, connectedness, and support.

The Word Family

What does the word *family* mean to you? What do family members mean to one another, and how do they express their connectedness? Share.

Memories of Home

Invite guests to share why they brought certain foods and symbols of home for the table.

Art as Meditation

Invite all those gathered to reflect for a time on the following poem by Letty Cottin Pogrebin:

> *If the family were a container, it would be a nest, an enduring nest,*
> *loosely woven, expansive, and open.*
> *If the family were a fruit, it would be an orange, a circle of sections,*
> *held together but separable—each segment distinct.*
> *If the family were a boat, it would be a canoe that makes no progress*
> *unless everyone paddles.*

If the family were a sport, it would be baseball: a long, slow, nonvio-
lent game that is never over until the last out.
If the family were a building, it would be an old but solid structure
that contains human history, and appeals to those who see the
carved moldings under all the plaster, the wide plank floors under
the linoleum, the possibilities.[1]

Hand out crayons or markers and paper. Ask volunteers to choose *one metaphor* in the poem and to draw a picture of it. After about fifteen minutes, spend some time talking together about the drawings.

C h o s e n   F a m i l y

Think about who the members are of the group that you would define as your "chosen family" (relatives and/or friends). How do they support you? How do you support them? Are there ways in which you would like to nurture certain persons more? Discuss.

S o u l - S h a r i n g

Marie Livingston Roy writes: "Jesus expressed a deeper bond of friendship when he called his disciples friends rather than servants. During their time together, Jesus and his disciples developed an intimate relationship, a soul-sharing that was based upon love rather than obligation."[2]

Whom do you trust enough to share your soul? Are there ways in which you could spend more time with these soul-sharing friends? Talk together.

T h e   M a k i n g   o f   R e l a t i v e s

Brooke Medicine Eagle explains:

One of the gifts White Buffalo Woman brought to the Lakota people was the rite of hunkapi, the making of relatives. And today, when we really care about someone and want to be close to them through our whole lives, we adopt them as relatives—as sister or brother or grandmother. I think this is what we're doing in our world right now—becoming relatives. Becoming family with each other in a whole new way.[3]

Whom have you adopted as relatives during your lifetime? What have these specially chosen people meant to you? Share with others what is comfortable.

The Person You Have Become
Author Natalie Goldberg has written:

These last two years . . . I don't have a great need for family any more, but I have an enormous number of friends, and I see my students and the people who work with me as being my family. I've created my own family, because the early vision I had of my family wouldn't allow me to be the Natalie Goldberg I am now.[4]

Who are the people in your circle who most allow you to be the person you have become? Reflect and share what is comfortable.

FOOD AS SYMBOL

This feast is a potluck in which everyone is invited to bring food that reminds them of home.

ELEVEN

THEME

This feast reminds us that each person has talents to share as it acknowledges that everyone's gifts are a valuable contribution toward the working of the whole.

REFLECTING TOGETHER: OPPORTUNITIES FOR DISCUSSION

(The leader selects those topics and activities that are most appropriate for the group and for which there is time. If children are present at this meal, include them in the conversation, using words they can easily understand.)

Quilts
It is suggested that the host procure a quilt or two for this event and articulate the symbolism of a quilt. (See "Creating the Environment.") This is a good opportunity to recognize the gifts of the quilt makers in the group as well.

The Story of the Candles and the Flame
Ask a guest to describe or read aloud a description of the candle centerpiece and what it signifies. (See "Setting the Table.")

Giftedness
What are your gifts? What do you do well, and what do you enjoy doing? Share your thoughts.

When have you felt as if your contributions were an important part of work that was done? Can you recall a particular occasion when you especially enjoyed completing a task with others? What did you do? How did that feel? Talk together.

How are your contributions of time, talent, and energy significant to your family? friends? faith community? job? volunteer work? other groups of which you are a part? Discuss.

SETTING THE TABLE—THE STORY OF THE CANDLES AND THE FLAME

A lovely and symbolic centerpiece for this event is a tray of candles of all different heights and widths. Just like the candles, we are all different: some younger, some older, some taller, some smaller; but each of us, regardless of size, has a gift to give. Even though the candles are varied, the size of the flame remains the same.

CREATING THE ENVIRONMENT

Quilts make excellent wall hangings for this event, or the host or hostess can use quilted table runners or any available quilted piece. A quilt is made up of individual pieces, which make up individual designs, which in turn make up the whole quilt. A quilt would not be a quilt if it were not made up of all those smaller parts working together.

FOOD AS SYMBOL

When we have company at our house, we enjoy the camaraderie of preparing a meal with our guests, because so much good visiting takes place during that process. Most people like to be included in the fixing stage and won't mind at all being asked to chop a vegetable or to stir a stew. Preparing a meal together promotes excellent community building and allows everyone to take ownership of the final product. We especially enjoy preparing Chinese stir-fry dishes with friends. These meals include much communal chopping, and we all enjoy making eggrolls from scratch.

The other night we were invited over to our friends' home and we had a ball making a big batch of delicious and elegant fondue. A fondue meal is especially entertaining because all the guests can bring a different kind of bread to be dipped. Fondue is also experiencing a dramatic comeback in popularity since the fondue frenzy of the 1960s. The following recipe for fondue can be doubled, tripled, or exponentially multiplied, and made in several pots.

FLEXIBLE, FANTASTIC FONDUE

1 pound grated Swiss, Gruyere, or Emmentaler cheese, or any combination thereof
3 tablespoons flour
1 or 2 cloves garlic
2 cups dry white wine
1 tablespoon lemon juice
2 tablespoons kirsch, dry sherry, or rum
1/8 teaspoon nutmeg (or to taste)
Cubed bread (approximately 2 loaves per pound of cheese)

Spray fondue pot or ceramic chafing dish with nonstick vegetable coating. Mix grated cheese with the flour. Rub the fondue pot or ceramic chafing dish with garlic. Pour in the wine and lemon juice and cook over moderate heat until wine begins to bubble. Add cheese by the handful, stirring constantly with a wooden spoon. When the cheese is melted, add the kirsch, rum, or sherry and the nutmeg. Stir over low heat until the fondue is very smooth. Regulate the heat so that the pot stays hot without boiling. Spear cubes of bread onto forks and dunk away. Serves 4.

The Story of Stone Soup

There is an old French tale called "Stone Soup," which is cleverly told and illustrated by American children's author Marcia Brown.[1] In this beloved story, three wandering soldiers dupe the selfish inhabitants of an entire town into showing hospitality by making soup that starts out with a few stones and a pot of water. Eventually all the townspeople bring ingredients to share. A huge pot of soup is made, and all consume a memorable feast—a feast made more significant by the fact that everyone shared and everyone took part.

A good stone soup option, especially if children are involved, is Corn and Hot Dog Chowder. Everybody can bring along a little something, and ingredients can be combined to taste. Experiment with your own stone soup recipes as well!

CORN AND HOT DOG CHOWDER

Creamed corn
Whole kernel corn
Half and half
Milk
Sliced hot dogs
A little bit of red bell pepper, chopped
A little bit of green bell pepper, chopped
A little bit of onion, chopped
Salt and pepper (to taste)

Combine ingredients. Cook uncovered over medium heat, stirring occasionally until thoroughly heated.

TWELVE

THEME

This is a feast that honors the fêted guest and bids us all to reflect on the meaning of life, wisdom, and age.

PLANNING AHEAD

In the birthday invitations, enclose 3 x 5-inch cards. Ask everyone to write an affirmation or a prayer of thanksgiving for the life of the honored guest and to bring these along to the celebration.

REFLECTING TOGETHER: OPPORTUNITIES FOR DISCUSSION

(The leader selects those topics and activities that are most appropriate for the group and for which there is time.)

Affirmations or Prayers of Thanksgiving
The host or hostess invites all present to read aloud their affirmations or prayers of thanksgiving for their friend's life. Each person shares aloud his or her written offering and places it in a box or bowl, which is then given to the birthday celebrant as a precious gift along with the loving messages. (The last time I participated in a birthday ritual, I found a beautiful inlaid

wood and abalone box from Egypt to give the birthday guest. This box along, with its tender messages, then became part of her personal altar.)

Life Story Circle
Have guests gather in a circle, ranking themselves in order according to how long they have known the honored guest (mothers, fathers, sisters, brothers, followed by childhood friends, etc.) Ask each guest to share how long he or she has known the birthday celebrant, the circumstances of their meeting, and their current connection. This lends a wonderful continuity to the celebration and honors the story of a life.[1] (This can be followed nicely by "Candles and Blessings.")

Candles and Blessings
At the end of the meal, the birthday cake is placed in the center of the room. Birthday candles are distributed to all the guests, including children. The host or hostess places on a table or stand near the cake a large, fat, white candle (the color white represents light and life) and lights it. One by one, each guest lights his or her smaller candle in the flame of the large candle of life, places it on the top of the birthday cake, and bestows a blessing on the birthday celebrant with the words, "I wish for you . . ." When every person has placed a candle on the cake and spoken a blessing, all hold hands in a large circle around the cake and sing "Happy Birthday."

A Young Soul
The thirteenth-century German mystic Meister Eckhart wrote:

> *My soul is as young as the day it was created.*
> *Yes, and much younger!*
> *In fact, I am younger today than I was yesterday,*
> *and if I am not younger tomorrow than I am today,*
> *I would be ashamed of myself.*

People who dwell in God dwell in the eternal now.
There, people can never grow old.
There, everything is present and everything is new.²

What does it mean to have a young soul? To dwell in the eternal now? To respond to everything as present and everything as new? Talk together.

Time Running toward Us

Russian physician and archbishop Anthony Bloom observes: "There is absolutely no need to run after time to catch it. It does not run away from us, it runs toward us."³

We always say, "I'm running out of time." Visualize time running *toward* you. How does that affect your understanding of what you want to do in your life? Share your thoughts.

SETTING THE TABLE

Try a group gift: Before the party, consider making a lovely tablecloth for the honored guest, which he or she can take home as a remembrance. Each friend could appliqué a symbol of the birthday celebrant's life, either by sewing or using fusible webbing and fabric paint. Or the host or hostess could hand out colorful permanent-ink fabric markers to guests, encouraging them to make a memorable tablecloth during the party.

FOOD AS SYMBOL

Ask the birthday celebrant to name his or her favorite foods and prepare those if possible.

Thirteen
LIVING IN THANKSGIVING: A FEAST OF GRATITUDE

THEME

This feast reminds us to live in a spirit of gratitude and thanksgiving each day.

PLANNING AHEAD

Encourage invited guests to bring their favorite food from the holiday of Thanksgiving or any favorite ethnic dish from their particular household. Ask guests also to bring a symbol of something for which they are particularly grateful. These could be objects from nature, family photos, special letters, books, etc. (See "Setting the Table.")

REFLECTING TOGETHER: OPPORTUNITIES FOR DISCUSSION

(The leader selects those topics and activities that are most appropriate for the group and for which there is time.)

Living in Gratitude
Who in your life taught you about living in gratitude? What effect has this had on you?

Opportunities for Growth
In 1 Thessalonians 5:18 we are reminded to "give thanks in all circumstances." Is this possible? Can we embrace the tragedies and the joys of our lives realizing that both provide oppor-

tunities for growth? Spend some time reflecting on your own life's circumstances and then share some thoughts in your group.

Food Memories

Talk about what each person has brought and what memories are associated with those particular foods.

Symbols of Gratitude

Allow some time during the celebration to have persons share their symbols of gratitude and explain why they chose those particular items.

Some Ideas Inspired by Author Christina Baldwin

1. *Reframing:* Christina Baldwin says, "Life is a great unending opportunity to see things differently, to keep reframing disaster and discouragement into faith."[1] Are you able to help yourself see things differently? Are you able to reframe disaster and discouragement into faith? Share what's comfortable.
2. *Blessing Obstacles:* Baldwin has a little exercise in her book *Life's Companion* called "Blessing Obstacles." She says, "When you hit an obstacle, write out everything good it is offering you. Bless it. Love it. Send it light."[2]

Look at your life right now. What obstacle, turning point, period of change are you going through at the present? Think about everything good it has to offer. Can you learn from this experience? Talk together.

3. *My Gift to the World:* Baldwin has also written an exercise called "A Gift a Day,"[3] which I have used over and over in my life—especially on those days that have seemed particularly frustrating or unproductive. Baldwin reminds us that we not only receive from the world each day, but we also give something back. She suggests that we think about one thing that we have contributed to the world today that we are willing to acknowledge as our gift. Then say to the world: "You're welcome."

What has the world to thank you for today? How might this exercise become a daily practice of self-affirmation in your life? Share your thoughts.

A Prayer of Thanksgiving

Author Kay Leigh Hagan writes:

> *Take time to notice areas of abundance in your life. Often scarcity, or the fear of scarcity, grabs our attention with urgency and crisis. Abundance is quiet, a presence that supports and nurtures us without demands. We may not realize the power that is available to us from abundance because of its lack of urgency. Your health, your chosen family, your training and experience, and your home are all areas that may give you consistent nurture through abundance.*[4]

Write a prayer of thanksgiving for your abundance, wherever that abundance makes itself known. Share your prayer aloud if you wish.

A L i t a n y o f T o a s t s

This litany of toasts, adapted from Psalm 148, may be shared before the meal as a blessing or during or after the meal to emphasize the theme of this feast of gratitude. This creation-centered time of toasting reminds me of Native American rituals thanking the Great Spirit for the interconnectedness of creation: all elements and forces, all things that live and breathe, all creatures, four-legged and two-legged.

Be sure to give everyone at the meal, children and adults alike, a glass to raise during this time of toasting. One way to get this started is to write down a few numbered toasts on strips of paper and slip them under random plates. When the time of toasting arrives, those with the slips of paper will stand, raise a glass, and shout loudly their phrase.

1. Praise God, all the angels!
2. Praise God, sun and moon!
3. Praise God, shining stars!
4. Praise God, highest heavens!
5. Praise God, sea monsters in the deeps!
6. Praise God, fire and hail!
7. Praise God, snow and frost!
8. Praise God, mountains and hills!
9. Praise God, fruit trees and cedars!
10. Praise God, wild animals and cattle!
11. Praise God, creeping things and flying birds!
12. Praise God, women and men!
13. Praise God, young and old!
14. Praise God, all peoples of the earth!

After the "assigned toasts" have been lifted, the leader may wish to invite other spontaneous exclamations beginning with "Praise God, . . . !" When all are finished, the leader may raise his or her glass to conclude the time of toasting with: "Praise God's name, God's glory is above heaven and earth!"

SETTING THE TABLE

This feast lends itself well to a thanksgiving centerpiece of some kind. Ask guests ahead of time to bring a symbol of something for which they are particularly grateful. These could be objects from nature, family photos, special letters, books, etc. These objects may be placed in decorative baskets or bowls or placed on a large table-length runner.

FOOD AS SYMBOL

Encourage guests to bring their favorite food from the holiday of Thanksgiving or any favorite ethnic dish from their particular household. A frequently prepared ethnic dish from our house is my husband's Chicken Curry.

Note: An excellent resource for this feast is *A Grateful Heart,* edited by M. J. Ryan. Excerpts from various chapters may be selected, read aloud, and talked about throughout the course of the feast.

JOHN WHITCOMB'S CHICKEN CURRY

1 whole fryer, cut up (about 3 pounds)
2 onions, diced
5 cloves garlic, minced
1 cup vegetable oil
3 tablespoons curry powder
1/2 cup boiling water
4 potatoes, diced
1 16-ounce bag frozen peas
4 tomatoes, diced
2 teaspoons salt (or to taste)
1 cup chopped fresh coriander (also called cilantro)
Sliced jalapeños (optional)

Fry the diced onions and the minced garlic in the oil until golden
brown. Mix the curry powder with the boiling water to form a slurry.
Spoon it into the onion and garlic. Fry 3–4 minutes until the oil "sep-
arates," stirring constantly to keep from burning. Add the chicken
pieces and sear in the spicy onion, garlic, and curry powder mix for
2–3 more minutes. Then add the potatoes, peas, tomatoes, and salt.
Simmer for 45 minutes. Serve over basmati or plain white rice.
Garnish with the fresh coriander and sliced jalapeños. (John says, "I
put 1 teaspoon of dried chilies in the frying onions and 3–4 sliced
jalapeños on top, and then I sweat a little.")

FOURTEEN

NATURE'S BOUNTY: A SUMMER PICNIC

THEME

This feast teaches us to appreciate and relish the majesty of nature.

PLANNING AHEAD

Ask guests to bring something to share that reminds them of the smells of summer.

REFLECTING TOGETHER: OPPORTUNITIES FOR DISCUSSION

(The leader selects those topics and activities that are most appropriate for the group and for which there is time.)

Good Openers (to Get to Know One Another Better)

1. *Smells of summer:*[1] Ask each person to pass around his or her "smells of summer" offering and to share why this smell is significant and what memories it evokes. Arrange the objects on a tray or in a basket as part of the summer picnic centerpiece. (See "Setting the Table.")

2. *Nature as teacher:* Go around the circle and share with the group a certain situation in your life in which some aspect of nature was your teacher.

3. *Animal medicine:* If you could be a nonhuman animal, what kind of animal would you be? What does this animal have to teach you? Talk together.

Things to Discuss or Do Later

1. *Soul as garden:* Teresa of Avila, the sixteenth-century Spanish mystic, describes the soul as a garden in which God delights to take rest.[2] How is your soul like a garden? What is growing abundantly and luxuriously? What needs a little more tending and nourishment to survive? Is there anything new you'd like to plant? Share your ideas.

2. *Planetary awareness:* Lie down on the ground and feel the contours of the earth beneath you. Look up at the sky. Take notice of what surrounds you. Sink into the ground and feel a oneness with the earth. Repeat this Navajo chant again and again until you feel the stirring truth of its words. Use a drum if you have one.

The Earth, its life am I,
The Earth, its feet are my feet,
The Earth, its legs are my legs,
The Earth, its body is my body,
The Earth, its thoughts are my thoughts,
The Earth, its speech is my speech.[3]

3. *Letter to the planet:* Journal writer Christina Baldwin suggests writing a love letter to the planet.[4] If you're comfortable with the idea, read your letters aloud.

4. *Praying a plant:* Approach a plant or tree of any kind and sit in receptive silence. Spend some time thinking about what it could tell you. Then spend some time reflecting on what you'd like to tell it. Don't rush. Enter fully into the experience.

5. *An orthodox walk:* This delightful term is borrowed from Tilden Edwards's *Living in the Presence.*[5] It means a walk during which you really pay attention to what's going on around you. Here are a couple of suggestions for meditation before embarking on an orthodox walk. The first is a reading from Meister Eckhart:

Apprehend God in all things,
for God is in all things.

Every single creature is full of God
and is a book about God.

Every creature is a word of God.

If I spent enough time with the tiniest creature—
even a caterpillar—

I would never have to prepare a sermon. So full of God
is every creature.[6]

Or you can use as your mantra this quotation from naturalist John Muir: "Every natural object is a conductor of divinity."[7] Say this phrase over and over again while you walk. Be attentive to the conductors of divinity all around you.

When you return from your walk, share with others what you have seen, heard, and reflected upon.

ART AS MEDITATION

The following recipes for fragrant summer take-home treats are adapted from a book called *Concoctions*.[8]

FLOWER POTPOURRI

Fragrant dried flowers and herbs, such as lilacs, roses, carnations, basil, rosemary, or mint
Fragrant spices such as allspice, cinnamon, or cloves
Rose oil or cinnamon oil
Small squares of nylon stockings or small squares of colorful gingham, cotton, or cheesecloth
Ribbon
Paper
Scissors
Hole punch
Fancy-colored marking pen (metallic gold is especially nice)

Combine the dried flowers, herbs, and spices in a large bowl. Add eight drops of rose oil or cinnamon oil and mix. Place a small amount of the dried mixture in the center of the square nylon or other cloth. Gather the sides of the cloth up around the potpourri and tie with ribbon. For a gift tag, cut out a small shape of paper, punch a hole in one corner, and tie one end of the ribbon through the hole. Write your message with the fancy marking pen.

This oil makes an attractive homemade gift. Those ornate vinegar bottles with corks make pretty containers. You may want to double or triple the recipe as long as you're getting everything together. I add glass marbles or seashells to the bottom of my jars for decoration.

SUMMER GARDEN BATH OIL

1 cup warm sunflower oil
Pine needles
Dried flowers (carnations, lilacs, roses, etc.)
16 (or more depending on how strong you like it) drops of oil of lavender, rose, or carnation
Cheesecloth
Rubber band
A piece of ribbon
1 plain jar
1 decorative bottle or jar

Put the warm oil into the plain jar. Add the pine needles and flowers and oil of lavender, rose, or carnation. Put the lid on the plain jar. Let the jar stand in a warm, sunny place for 24 hours in the summer or 36 hours in the winter. Take off the lid. Cover the mouth of the jar with the cheesecloth and hold tight with the rubber band. Pour the mixture through the cheesecloth into the decorative bottle or jar. Tie a ribbon around the neck of the decorative container. Use the oil in your bath or as a light scent directly on your body.

SETTING THE TABLE

Place a colorful picnic cloth on the ground or on the table. Create an appealing centerpiece after the smells of summer offerings are presented and discussed. (See "Reflecting Together.") Freshly picked flowers or a bowl of colorful vegetables would also be attractive.

FOOD AS SYMBOL

Any succulent, fresh summer food that celebrates the glory of the season is appropriate. During the summer, I like to greet my guests with simple strawberry yogurt shakes. Put plain or vanilla yogurt and fresh or frozen strawberries in a blender. Add sugar or sugar substitute. Blend. Pour into large goblets.

One option for this Summer Picnic is my simple summer gazpacho. On a hot day, this can be a meal in itself when served with fresh bread and butter.

REFRESHING SUMMER GAZPACHO

8 cups V-8 juice
4 cups diced tomatoes
2 cups minced sweet green pepper
2 diced cucumbers
6 finely chopped scallions
2 crushed cloves garlic
3/4 cup chopped coriander (also called cilantro)
2 teaspoons honey
juice of one lemon
juice of one lime
4 tablespoons wine vinegar
4 tablespoons olive oil
1/4 teaspoon ground cumin
salt and pepper (to taste)
tabasco (to taste)

Combine all ingredients. Chill for at least 2 hours. Serves 8.

I love big fresh salads in the summer. The following salad with an Asian flair is one of my favorites.

CRUNCHY SESAME COLESLAW

Dressing:
2 tablespoons soy sauce
1 seasoning packet from Ramen noodles
3/4 cup oil
2 tablespoons vinegar
4 tablespoons sugar
1/2 teaspoon black pepper

Crunchies:
4 tablespoons sesame seeds
4 ounces sliced almonds
2 3-ounce packages Ramen noodles
1–2 tablespoons butter

Salad:
1-pound bag coleslaw mix or 8 cups shredded cabbage
6 scallions, chopped

Whisk together dressing ingredients in large bowl. Chop scallions and prepare coleslaw mix or cabbage. Toss with dressing. Sauté sesame seeds and sliced almonds in 1–2 tablespoons butter. Toss into salad. Add crushed Ramen noodles right before serving.

The following strawberry cream cheese spread is lovely when fresh strawberries are in season. It's delicious on nut bread. (See chapter 17, "Tea and Sabbath," for Rich Date Nut Bread.)

STRAWBERRY CREAM CHEESE SPREAD

8 ounces cream cheese, softened
1/3 cup powdered sugar
3/4 cup sliced strawberries

Mix together and refrigerate.

A pleasing seasonal dessert is fresh fruit and whipped cream, or blueberry, strawberry, or peach shortcake.

Note: An excellent resource for planning this feast is Joseph Cornell's *Listening to Nature.* Excerpts may be selected, read aloud, experienced, and talked about throughout the course of this summer picnic.

FIFTEEN
TRUSTING AND WAITING: A WINTER PICNIC

THEME

This feast examines the theme of gestation: Just as a seed gestates deep in the soil in winter, some of our qualities need to be tended with care while we wait faithfully and patiently.

REFLECTING TOGETHER: OPPORTUNITIES FOR DISCUSSION

(The leader selects those topics and activities that are most appropriate for the group and for which there is time.)

Waiting and Patience

Winter is cold, and gestation is about waiting and patience. Author Maria Harris says that "even though . . . parts of ourselves are still underground, our spirituality is taking root, growing, and pushing through to life. In its own time, when the pregnancy is completed, it will emerge from hiddenness. Meanwhile, every day of our lives we can learn to feel where life is emerging from similar hiddenness."[1]

What has taken root in you that needs time and patience for further growth? How might you best make use of waiting to nurture the life that may spring forth? Talk together.

The poet John Soos expresses a similar image:

To be of the Earth is to know
the restlessness of being a seed
the darkness of being planted
the struggle toward the light
the pain of growth into the light
the joy of bursting and bearing fruit
the love of being food for someone
the scattering of your seeds
the decay of the seasons
the mystery of death
and the miracle of birth.[2]

What comes to mind when you read this poem? What does this poem say about your life? Share.

Gestation's Helpers

One of the definitions of gestation in Webster's unabridged dictionary is an "exercise in which one is borne or carried." Are you being borne or carried? Who is bearing you or carrying you? Could God be active as the Bearer or Carrier of your own birthing process? Could God be one who helps you give birth to yourself?

The thirteenth-century mystic Meister Eckhart reflected:

> *The seed of God is in us.*
> *Now*
> > > *the seed of a pear tree*
> > > > *grows into a pear tree;*
> > > *and a hazel seed*
> > > > *grows into a hazel tree;*
>
> > *a seed of God*
> > > *grows into*
>
> > > *God.*[3]

What does this poem mean to you? Does it say anything about your own gestating and birthing process? Discuss.

ART AS MEDITATION

Underground Riches

Draw the surface of the ground as a line in the middle of a piece of paper and draw the sun up in the sky. Below the surface of the ground, draw the seeds you have planted. Name the seeds and draw the seeds' root systems if there are any. What are the names of your seeds?

Now examine the root systems. Who or what make up the supportive systems for each one of your seeds? Reflect upon your seeds. What do they need to flourish and grow?

Are there any weeds starting to sprout among the roots? If so, draw the weeds. Who or what are the weeds choking your growth?

After you have drawn your picture, if you're comfortable doing so, share with the others what it represents to you.

Symbolic Plantings

Each person places some soil in a small pot or paper cup, plants an easy-to-grow seed or bean, and waters it. Then each person talks about what this particular planting might represent in his or her life. Guests are invited to keep these small plantings as symbols of the constant gestation and invitation to careful nurture that is taking place in each one of us.

CREATING THE ENVIRONMENT

The setting for this meal is a joyous winter picnic simulating as many of the genuine smells and memories of summer as possible. If you have a fireplace, build a roaring fire. If you don't, fix up a tray of votive candles or big lighted pillar candles of all different heights. Throw a red-and-white-checked tablecloth or picnic blanket on the floor.

FOOD AS SYMBOL

As mentioned previously, try to make the atmosphere and the food for the Winter Picnic as summery as possible. Serve hot dogs or hamburgers and chips. If possible, toast marshmallows or make s'mores. You may even want to get the outside grill fired up for this special occasion. Fix the food yourself or ask everyone to bring something summery for a potluck.

SIXTEEN

THEME

This feast celebrates women and their foremothers, as well as the collective wisdom of women through the ages. (Note: Although the chapter is written assuming only women will participate, those planning this feast might want to adapt it to include any men wishing to join in honoring their foremothers.)

PLANNING AHEAD

Ask each woman invited to bring a dish that a woman family member or mentor taught her to prepare and copies of the recipe to share.

If you choose Option 1, "A woman remembered," in the roll call of the saints (see "Reflecting Together"), enclose 3 x 5-inch cards in the invitations. Ask each guest to write a short paragraph about a woman mentor, explaining why she has been a role model. Ask guests to bring these with them to the feast.

REFLECTING TOGETHER: OPPORTUNITIES FOR DISCUSSION

(The leader selects those topics and activities that are most appropriate for the group and for which there is time.)

Introductions

The women sit in a circle. Ask a guest to read the following quotations.

Author and theologian Kathleen Fischer writes:

We are linked not only physically, but spiritually as well, to our mothers, our grandmothers, and all the women who have come before us. With them we share a common gender identity and the social roles and expectations that go with it.[1]

In writing about the Motherline, author Ruth Naomi Lowinsky says,

Envision the word line as a cord, a thread, as the yarn emerging from the fingers of a woman at the spinning wheel. Imagine cords of connection tied over generations. Like weaving or knitting, each thread is tied to others to create a complex, richly textured cloth connecting the past to the future.[2]

Each woman introduces herself by saying her own name, then naming her mother, her grandmothers, and the states or countries they have come from. For example: "I am Naomi of California, daughter of Giesele of Germany, granddaughter of Emma of Germany and Clara of Russia."[3]

When the first woman is finished introducing herself in this way, she is given a ball of yarn. She then holds an end of the yarn in her hand and throws the ball of yarn to another woman in the circle. The woman who has caught the ball of yarn introduces herself through her women's lineage, again holds a piece of the yarn and then gently throws the ball of yarn to someone else. When every woman has spoken and this visual image of a connecting web has been created, take time to comment on these women's lineages and the theme of connected lives, experiences, and expectations. Then drop the web to the floor and invite the women to clip off pieces to take home so that they may have a tangible reminder of these connected lives and this passed-on wisdom.

Roll Call of the Saints
Option 1. A woman remembered: (See "Planning Ahead.") An example of such a short paragraph would be:

> *I remember my grandmother Kathryn Wilson who baby-sat me when I was little so both of my parents could go to work. She taught me the art of playfulness and a love of laughter as we lay giggling together for an hour in what was supposed to be my nap time. My grandmother Kathryn loved me unconditionally and taught me the true meaning of acceptance and nurture.*

Invite each woman to stand one at a time and share her tribute of a loved one, mentor, or friend, of a Nana, Auntie, Mum, or Grandma. End this time by standing in a circle holding hands. Repeat line by line after the leader:

> *We remember this cloud of witnesses, (repeat)*
> *these women who have inspired us (repeat)*
> *and given us courage. (repeat)*
> *These women have taught us what we needed to know (repeat)*
> *in order to survive. (repeat)*
> *We offer thanks (repeat)*
> *that these lives have touched our own. (repeat)*

Option 2: Women who have been my teachers: In numerous cultures, the lineage of ancestors or spiritual teachers has traditionally come through the male. This time of celebration and reflection invites women to claim their lineage of wise women. Invite each woman to stand, to say a few words about her chosen teacher, and to close her tribute by saying, "[Name], you have been my teacher, I honor you."

If the leader wishes to add a little drama to this ritual, she can buy as many freshly cut flowers as she has guests. She places the cut flowers in a pile next to a large vase. As each woman names and honors her own esteemed teacher, she chooses one of the cut flowers and places it in the vase. As all the wise women teachers are recalled, their collective memory is symbolized in the grandeur of a lush bouquet.

Option 3: Women who were standing before us: Play a recording of Carole Etzler Eagleheart's powerful song "Standing before Us."[4] Stop the recording between verses and call out the names of women mentors.

Option 4: Reserving a place at our table and in our hearts: (This could also fall under the category of "Setting the Table.") This exercise is borrowed from author Maria Harris, who received her inspiration from Judy Chicago's The Dinner Party:

> *If the group is large, form into small groups of no more than five or six.*
>
> *Each group is given a paper placemat and some crayons or paint materials (or more elaborate materials if that is possible).*
>
> *Each group is then asked to choose one woman—well known, little known, or virtually unknown—whose Memory they wish to celebrate.*
>
> *Each group is then given thirty to forty minutes to design a placemat for that woman.*

At the end of the period, the placemats are put on tables that have already been set with glasses, napkins, and cutlery. The meal begins with the toasting of the women who are being remembered, and with a brief commentary on [that] woman's life, for example:

> *"We wish to toast Rosa Parks, a woman of courage who showed all women the meaning of human dignity by her refusal to obey an unjust, racist law, a woman who stands as a role model for women in the continuing work of justice," to which all respond: "To Rosa Parks!"*[5]

Beloved Woman's Recipe

Take time to share at the table what food each guest brought and where she learned the recipe. Distribute copies of the recipes.

A Grandmother Story

Have every woman take turns telling a favorite story or reminiscence about her grandmother or one who acted as a grandmother.[6]

Women Breaking Out

Think of the women in your family: your mothers, your grandmothers, your great-grandmothers, aunts, or other women who played significant roles in your growing up. What cultural and familial and societal expectations held them down? How did they exhibit courage? How did they inspire you? Talk together.

Now think of yourself: What cultural or familial or societal expectations have held you down? How have you been courageous or inspiring to your daughters, nieces, granddaughters, or any other younger women around you? Discuss.

Womanriver Flowing On
Sit in a circle quietly and listen to Carole Etzler Eagleheart's song "Womanriver Flowing On."[7]
Reflect as a group on what this song has to say about your sense of connectedness with other
women.

FOOD AS SYMBOL

Encourage each woman to bring a dish that a woman family member or mentor taught her to
prepare as well as copies of the recipe to share.

PART 2

Culinary

Interludes

REFLECTIONS PLANNED AROUND FOOD, BUT NOT ENTIRE FEASTS

Seventeen

THEME

This interlude helps us understand the biblical concept of Sabbath as a time of renewal, rest, and reconnection with God within the context of a relaxed and tranquil time of tea.

INTRODUCTION

I married a man who was raised in India as the child of American church workers. Much to my delight, my parents-in-law have always celebrated tea in the British and Indian traditions. Whenever we are with them, we always pause for tea around ten o'clock in the morning and again around four o'clock in the afternoon. How refreshingly civilized to stop in this way and allow oneself welcome pauses for refreshment, renewal, and conversation! I have also come to relish the delicious hot drink called chai, Indian tea boiled with milk and cardamom.

Tea has always represented a sacred pause in the busy routines of our lives, whether observed as British high tea or as the Zen tea master celebrates *cha-no-yu*, the Japanese ceremony of drinking tea. One writer has said, "Tea drinking is the art of being truly present with each other and the situation, sensitive to the sacred qualities of everything."[1]

When I had the opportunity recently to participate in a genuine Japanese tea ceremony at my local natural history museum, we were told, "The tea ceremony teaches us how to focus our attention on balance, giving weight to lighter concerns and lightness to heavier concerns." D. T. Suzuki says, "A fire is made, water is boiled, and tea is served: this is all that is needed here, no other worldly considerations are to intrude." Suzuki asks, "Who would deny that when I am sipping tea in my tearoom I am swallowing the whole universe with it and that this very moment of my lifting the bowl to my lips is eternity itself transcending time and space?"[2] It is appropriate to link together the hallowed and mystical observance of tea with the sacred observance of the Sabbath.

UNDERSTANDING SABBATH

The Sabbath is observed fully by Orthodox and Conservative Jews and less stringently by Reform Jews and by Christians. In the Jewish tradition, Sabbath is observed from sunset on Friday to sunset on Saturday. To most Christians, Sunday is the day of Sabbath, the day of resurrection. The term Sabbath goes back to the creation story as told in the Old Testament. This story tells us that God created the world in six days and on the seventh day God rested. This seventh day of God's rest and simultaneous and continuing creation was called the Sabbath. *Sabbath* comes from the Hebrew word *Shabbat*, which means "rest." Hear the words of the Sabbath commandment in Exodus 20:8–11:

> *Remember the sabbath day, to keep it holy. Six days you shall labor and do all your work; but the seventh day is a sabbath to the Sovereign your God; in it you shall not do any work, you, or your son, or your daughter, or your manservant, or your womanservant, or your cattle, or the resident alien who is within your gates; for in six days God made heaven and earth, the sea, and all that is in them, and rested the seventh day; therefore God blessed the sabbath day and hallowed it.[3]*

It is important to remember that Sabbath rest is more than an indulgence; it is a law. In the Old Testament, Sabbath is taken so seriously that violating the law of Sabbath is equal

to breaking all of the law.[4] Sabbath is a commandment to rest. It is a commandment to celebrate the givenness of our most basic identity as people of God. Isaiah 43:1 says, "I have called you by name, you are mine." Sabbath celebrates the love God has for us and God's grace which sustains us from day to day. We don't earn God's love; it is given. We need Sabbath rest to ponder and internalize this truth.

When her theology students asked professor and educator Maria Harris to define the rules of Sabbath, she explained, "It is a not-doing. Rest means doing nothing, doing no thing. It means being receptive: to yourself and to others, to sorrow as well as joy. It means cultivating the ability to sit still in a room. Once again 'sometimes ah sets and thinks,' says the wise old woman, 'and sometimes ah jes sets.'"[4]

Molly Cone, an author who tries to explain the idea of Sabbath to young children, says, "On the Jewish Sabbath, it is against the law to mourn. And against the law to worry. And against the law to *work*." In explaining further that the Sabbath literally means the word *rest*, Cone explains, "Some people rest by walking, or visiting, or reading, or playing. Rest means being free to just *be*."[5]

One of the foremost scholars who has written on the subject of Sabbath is a rabbi by the name of Abraham Heschel. Here are a few assorted quotations from Heschel's classic book, *The Sabbath*.[6] See which of these quotations speaks most clearly to your experience of Sabbath rest. Ask several persons to take turns reading aloud, each sharing a quotation from Heschel.

The meaning of the Sabbath is to celebrate time rather than space. Six days a week we live under the tyranny of things of space; on the Sabbath we try to become attuned to holiness in time. It is a day on which we are called upon to share in what is eternal in time, to turn from the results of creation to the mystery of creation; from the world of creation to the creation of the world.

The Sabbath is not for the sake of the weekdays; the weekdays are for the sake of Sabbath. It is not an interlude but the climax of living.

Labor is a craft, but perfect rest is an art. It is the result of an accord of body, mind and imagination. . . . The seventh day is a palace in time *which we build.*

To observe the Sabbath is to celebrate the coronation of a day in the spiritual wonderland of time.

The Sabbath is not dedicated exclusively to spiritual goals. It is a day of the soul as well as of the body; comfort and pleasure are an integral part of the Sabbath observance.

The work on weekdays and the rest on the seventh day are correlated. The Sabbath is the inspirer, the other days the inspired.

REFLECTING TOGETHER: OPPORTUNITIES FOR DISCUSSION

(Leader picks out those topics and activities which are most appropriate for the group and for which there is time.)

Heschel Quotations

Which of the quotations from Rabbi Abraham Heschel spoke to you the most profoundly? Why?

Sabbath: Definition

Brainstorm for a moment and share aloud what words immediately come to your mind when you hear the word Sabbath.

Sabbath as Re-creation

Are you currently observing the Sabbath in your life? What is your own experience of Sabbath? Are there acts of re-creation that keep you connected with God and with the rest of humankind? (Mine are leisurely hot baths and long walks.) Discuss.

Sabbath as Commandment

Can you remind yourself that in the Judeo-Christian tradition Sabbath is no less than a law? Do you need to give yourself permission to observe the Sabbath with more life-giving frequency? How might this feel? How might this happen? Talk together.

Sabbath and Discernment

Sabbath is an ideal time to reflect and ask for God's wisdom and to be open to a process of discernment. Author Marjorie Thompson says, "Discernment is a process of seeking guidance from God concerning what is true, good, or divinely willed in an ambiguous situation. Life is full of 'wheat and tares' growing together, so much so that it is often hard to distinguish between what is healthy food and what looks good but cannot yield nourishment."[7]

What important decisions are you in the midst of making right now? At what turning point in life do you find yourself? How might you invite God during a time of Sabbath rest to be a part of the decision-making process that lies before you? Share your ideas.

Final Blessing

When you have reflected on several of the above exercises, conclude teatime together by blessing each other with the words "Good rest! Good Sabbath!"

FOOD AS SYMBOL

Create a celebrative and relaxed teatime for yourself and a few friends. Remove crusts from your favorite sliced bread, fill with sandwich spread, and cut with cookie cutters; or just buy some cookies or crackers and cheese from the store. If you have the time and if you're in a really festive mood, try a few of our family's favorite teatime recipes, starting with my husband's *chai*—the genuine article.

JOHN WHITCOMB'S INDIAN TEA: CHAI

Boil a mixture of half water and half *whole* milk. Add 1 tea bag for each 2 cups of liquid. Boil the tea bags for 4–5 minutes at a low simmer. Add lots of sugar—about 1 tablespoon per cup. Garnish with a trace of cardamom; about 2 or 3 cardamom pods per pot is ideal.

LEMON CREAM WITH MACAROONS

1 6-ounce can frozen lemonade, thawed
1 8-ounce carton whipped topping
1 14-ounce can sweetened condensed milk
2 drops yellow food coloring
1 pound soft, chewy coconut macaroons (homemade or purchased)

Mix thawed lemonade, whipped topping, sweetened condensed milk, and food coloring. Break the macaroons into little pieces. Set aside one cup broken macaroons. Line the bottom of a 13 x 9-inch pan with the larger quantity of macaroon pieces. Fold the remaining 1 cup of macaroon pieces into the lemon cream. Spoon the lemon cream into macaroon crust. Cover and freeze at least 4 hours until firm. Cut frozen mixture into small squares as it is very rich. Serves 15–20.

I like to make the following recipe for my father-in-law, because it reminds him of the hearty and moist bread his mother used to make.

RICH DATE NUT BREAD

Date and nut mixture:
1 10-ounce package chopped, pitted dates
2 cups chopped walnuts
1/2 stick melted butter
1/4 teaspoon baking soda
1/4 teaspoon salt
1/2 cup coffee (in liquid form)

Batter:
2 eggs
1 teaspoon vanilla
1 1/2 cups flour
3/4 cup firmly packed brown sugar
1 1/2 teaspoons baking powder

Preheat oven to 350 degrees. Grease an 8 x 4-inch loaf pan, a round layer-cake pan, or an 8- or 9-inch square pan. To make the batter, mix eggs with vanilla, then add flour, sugar, and baking powder. Prepare the date and nut mixture by combining all the ingredients; add to the batter. Pour into the greased pan. Bake 50–60 minutes. Do not overbake. Center should be slightly moist. If you're using a loaf pan, cool completely before removing.

EASY CHEESE DANISH

2 cans crescent rolls

Filling:
3 8-ounce packages cream cheese, softened
1 cup sugar
2 egg yolks
1 1/2 teaspoons vanilla

Topping:
1 egg white, beaten until foamy
1/4 cup sugar
1/2 cup crushed walnuts

Spread 1 can crescent rolls on the bottom of an ungreased
13 x 9-inch pan. Beat together cream cheese, sugar, egg yolks,
and vanilla. Spread on bottom crust. Place second can of crescent
rolls over the top, pressing sides and middle together. Spoon or
brush egg white mixture on top. Sprinkle with sugar and walnuts.
Bake at 350 degrees for 30 minutes. Serves 10.

EIGHTEEN

THEME

This culinary interlude probes the heart as the source of inner insight.

REFLECTING TOGETHER: OPPORTUNITIES FOR DISCUSSION

(The leader selects those topics and activities that are most appropriate for the group and for which there is time.)

A Diversity of Hearts

The enlarged heart: Psalm 119:32 (KJV) says, "I will run the way of thy commandments, when thou shalt enlarge my heart." Medically, the idea having of an enlarged heart is terrifying, but metaphorically, it is deeply satisfying. When in your life have you felt filled or motivated or inspired, as if your heart were truly enlarged? For what purpose might you wish an enlarged heart? Share your thoughts.

In a selection from *Prayers for a Planetary Pilgrim*, Edward Hays prays, "Broaden the boundaries of my heart that it may encompass more than it did yesterday."[1] What are some ways in which you might enlarge your heart by broadening the boundaries of your heart? How could this change the way you live from day to day?

The moist heart: Maria Harris says, in *Dance of the Spirit*, "Native Americans describe spirituality as having a 'moist heart,' perhaps because native wisdom knows the soil of the

123

human heart is necessarily watered with tears, and that tears keep the ground soft. From such ground new life is born."[2] What are the advantages of living with a "moist heart"? Are there times when you have had a more moist heart than at other times? Why was this so? Discuss.

The listening heart: Mystics throughout the ages have listened with their hearts as they become more and more attentive to God's will. Do you have a listening heart? What are you hearing with your heart these days? Share.

The seeing heart: In the beloved classic *The Little Prince,* writer Antoine de Saint-Exupéry shares this wisdom through the mouth of the fox: "And now here is my secret, a very simple secret: It is only with the heart that one can see rightly; what is essential is invisible to the eye."[3] As you reflect on your life, in what circumstances have you seen with your heart instead of your eyes? Where has this "seeing heart" led you? What are the benefits of seeing with your heart? Talk together.

The generous heart: A Nigerian proverb says, "It is the heart that gives; the fingers just let go." What is your heart open to giving? How does this heart generosity make you feel? What is your heart closed to giving? How does this affect you? What might you like to change? Discuss.

The mind that is in the heart: Writers in the Eastern Christian tradition name the heart as being the center of the personality and admonish believers to "put the mind in the heart." A nineteenth-century bishop, Theophan the Recluse, describes the purpose of Christian prayer this way: "The principal thing is to stand before God with the mind in the heart, and go on standing before [God] unceasingly day and night until the end of life."[4] How might your life be different if you stood before God with your mind in your heart? Is there a dichotomy between heart and mind in your life? What would it mean to lead with your heart? Share your thoughts.

A R T   A S   M E D I T A T I O N

Draw a picture of a big heart that represents your own heart.[5] Take a few minutes to sit quietly and ponder what is in your heart these days. Draw it as well as you can. If you wish, add words to the drawing. Don't rush. Be honest. Depict the negative as well as the positive. What did you learn from taking this time to draw? If you feel comfortable doing so, talk about it.

Now picture the heart of God. Sit quietly and reflect on what this might mean. Draw the heart of God. Add words if you wish. What did you learn from doing this? How is God's heart different from your own? If you're comfortable doing so, talk about what you drew.

F O O D   A S   S Y M B O L

Heart-shaped food of almost any kind would be appropriate for this culinary interlude: candies, cake, cookies, little breads, finger gelatin cut with heart cookie cutters. How about spooning the Strawberry Cream Cheese recipe from the summer picnic (chapter 14) into a heart-shaped mold? Be open to various possibilities depending on the occasion and time of day. If you're in a hurry, ready-to-bake sugar-cookie dough purchased in a refrigerated roll is delicious and quick. Roll out dough, cut with a heart-shaped cookie cutter, and bake in the oven. Cool and frost with pink canned frosting or a powdered-sugar frosting made from scratch.

To make heart lollipop cookies (both adults and children love these), insert a wooden craft stick in the dough before baking. These are cute and a little different. When my children were small, they always asked me to make these for their birthday parties at school.

For a fancy dessert, bake a decadent cheesecake or rich chocolate cake in a heart-shaped pan. Or try a chocolate cheesecake heart.

CHOCOLATE CHEESECAKE HEART IN COOKIE CRUST

1 1/2 cups finely crushed, cream-filled sandwich cookies
1/4 cup margarine or butter, melted
1 8-ounce package cream cheese, softened
1 14-ounce can sweetened condensed milk
1 cup (6 ounces) semi-sweet chocolate chips, melted
2 eggs
1 teaspoon vanilla

Preheat oven to 350 degrees. Combine finely crushed cookies and melted margarine or butter. Pat into the bottom and up the sides of an 8 1/2-inch heart-shaped pan. In bowl, beat cream cheese until fluffy. Add sweetened condensed milk and the melted chocolate chips. Stir in eggs and vanilla. Pour into crust and bake about 35 minutes or until set in middle. Chill. Garnish with whipped cream and fresh strawberries or chocolate hearts. Serves 8 – 10.

Nineteen

THEME

This culinary interlude focuses on our "peak" experiences and encourages us to recall those experiences for personal growth.

UNDERSTANDING THE MOUNTAINTOP PERSPECTIVE

When I was a child, each summer my parents took me and my sister on camping trips to the Rocky Mountains of Colorado or the Snowy Range of Wyoming. We often camped at high altitudes and planned long day hikes on which we could climb to the summit of one peak or another. I remember that feeling of being on top of the world—that exhausted exhilaration of seeing only clouds above and everything else below. Being on the mountaintop alters one's perspective. You can come back down the mountain, but you are never quite the same.

REFLECTING TOGETHER: OPPORTUNITIES FOR DISCUSSION

(The leader selects those topics and activities that are most appropriate for the group and for which there is time.)

Guided Imagery: View from the Top

Leader (very slowly so as to provide ample time for reflection between phrases): Close your eyes. Relax. Take a few deep breaths, in and out . . . Imagine that you have reached the top of a mountain. Sit down and rest. Look around in all directions: What do you see? What do you feel? How is this experience affecting your perspective? When you feel ready to come back from the mountain, slowly open your eyes again.

Guided Imagery: Overview of Peak Experiences

Leader (very slowly so as to provide ample time for reflection between phrases): Close your eyes. When you think of peak experiences in your life, what immediately comes to mind? Go back to your childhood. What was a peak experience during those years? Now reflect on your teenage years: What peak experiences occurred at that time? Finally, think about your adult years. Reflect on one or two peak experiences for each ten years. Take some time to remember these things (allow several minutes). When you feel ready, slowly open your eyes and focus your attention back into this room.

Some Quotations to Consider
On April 3, 1968—the day before he was assassinated—Dr. Martin Luther King Jr., at a church in Memphis, Tennessee, delivered one of his greatest speeches. In the closing paragraph of that speech, Dr. King said: "I've been to the mountaintop. . . . And I've looked over. And I've seen the promised land."[1]

What mountaintop experience have you had in your life that has given you a hint of your promised land? How did this change your life? Talk together.

Now consider the following quotation from Ram Dass:

After one arrives at the summit, after going through the total transformation of being . . . there is yet one more step to the completion of that journey: the return to the valley below, to the everyday world. Who it is that returns is not who began the climb in the first place. The being that comes back is quietness itself, is compassion and wisdom, is the truth of the ages. Whatever humble or elevated position that being holds within the community, he or she becomes a light for others on the way, a statement of freedom that comes from having touched the top of the mountain.[2]

What peak experience have you had that has enabled you to become for others a light along the way? Share.

Finally, consider the following quotation from Todd Smelser:

The mystery of sacramental life is not that we can hold onto these holy, life-giving moments, these mountain top experiences forever—but rather that we are changed by them, and the world becomes a different place for us—a safer, more loving, more remarkable place. We undergo transfiguration, and our lives are molded and re-created by the power of God's love.[3]

What peak experience have you had that has made you feel that the world is a safer and more loving place? Discuss.

FOOD AS SYMBOL

It is suggested that food eaten during this culinary interlude or dessert time be somewhat mountaintop-like in appearance. Your favorite recipe for Baked Alaska would be excellent, or if you want to try others, consider the following.

M O U N T A I N T O P   T O R T E

1 pound chopped dates
1/2 cup sugar
1/2 cup flour
1 teaspoon baking powder
1 teaspoon vanilla
1 cup chopped pecans or walnuts
4 eggs
1 16-ounce can crushed pineapple, drained
1 15-ounce can mandarin oranges, drained
2 sliced bananas
For garnish, any of the following: fresh orange sections, fresh strawberries,
fresh sliced peaches, or maraschino cherries (drained)

Combine first seven ingredients and bake in a greased 9 x 13-inch
pan at 350 degrees until done, about 30 minutes. Let cake cool.
Tear cake up into 1-inch pieces and add the drained pineapple, the
drained mandarin oranges, and the sliced bananas. Press into a
round, medium-sized mixing bowl; cover; and chill overnight.
Unmold and frost with whipped topping or sweetened whipped
cream. Garnish with fresh fruit or maraschino cherries. Drizzle with
melted chocolate. Refrigerate 1–2 hours or more before serving.
Refrigerate leftovers.

I recently served the following cake at a wedding anniversary celebration. It was a hit.

RASPBERRY SUMMIT CAKE

1 angel food cake, homemade or purchased
1 small jar raspberry preserves (whatever flavor of preserves you have around
will probably do fine)
1 pint raspberry sherbet, softened
1 16-ounce tub whipped topping or whipped cream
Optional garnish: fresh fruit or shaved chocolate

Carefully, with a long, serrated knife, cut off a 1-inch section from
the top of the cake. Gingerly set aside. Hollow out a tunnel leaving
1-inch walls and bottom. Spread the preserves over the bottom and
sides of the tunnel. Fill with raspberry sherbet. With care, replace
the top of cake. At this point, if you are not serving the cake immediately, wrap it and freeze. When ready to serve, frost liberally with
whipped topping. Fresh fruit or shaved chocolate may be sprinkled
on top.

TWENTY

THEME

This culinary interlude includes diverse reflections on spirituality that take place within a process of making and breaking bread together. The concept of this bread-making experience is adapted from the work of Darlene Christiansen.[1]

PLANNING AHEAD AND FOOD AS SYMBOL

In this particular experience, a number of people make poppy seed bread together. Group discussion or personal note-taking accompanies each step of the preparation. After the participants mix and place in the oven the batter for the two (or more) loaves, they cut and share two (or more) loaves baked ahead of time. The bread may be eaten with hot coffee, iced tea, or whatever is appropriate to the season and time of day.

POPPY SEED BREAD

3 eggs
2/3 cup oil
1 1/4 cups evaporated milk
1 1/2 teaspoons lemon or almond extract
2 1/4 cups flour
1 1/2 cups sugar
3/4 cup poppy seed
4 1/2 teaspoons baking powder

Preheat oven to 350 degrees (325 degrees if you are using glass pans). Grease and flour two 9 x 5-inch loaf pans. Beat eggs in mixing bowl. Add oil, milk, lemon or almond extract. Beat well. Stir in dry ingredients until batter is smooth. Pour batter into pans and bake until toothpick inserted comes out clean, about 45–50 minutes.

REFLECTING TOGETHER: OPPORTUNITIES FOR DISCUSSION

Introduction to Making Bread

Go around a circle and share: Have you ever received some kind of loaf of bread as a gift or have you ever given some kind of loaf as a gift? On what occasion? Talk together. (As stated previously in the introduction to this book, the word *companion* comes from the Latin and means literally "one with whom bread is broken.")

Making Bread Together

Directions to leader: Sustain momentum from one part to another: there are eleven steps in all. If there are no more comments, move on. Take more time with those sections in which there seems to be a natural interest.

Step 1: Heating the oven. Preheat the oven to 350 degrees. We've all heard the old adage, "If you can't stand the heat, get out of the kitchen." What factors are causing heat in your life right now? What stresses are you experiencing? What steps could you take to control the heat, to cope a little better with some of those stresses? Jot down a few notes for yourself.

Step 2: Preparing the loaf pans. Grease and flour the pans so that the dough won't stick. Can you recall times in which your belief in God or your various emotional support systems have prepared you to handle a sticky situation? Discuss.

Step 3: Breaking and beating eggs. An egg is a symbol of new life. What new life do you yearn to add to your existence? Discuss.

Step 4: Adding oil. Oil serves as the fat in this recipe. We usually think of fat as something evil to be taken off by exercise or diet. But in some recipes fat is necessary. Fat creates a more tender product. Fat holds ingredients together, as in a pie crust. Who are the people who are helping you to hold your life together right now? What qualities in these persons do you appreciate? Discuss.

Step 5: Adding evaporated milk. Evaporated milk serves as the liquid in this recipe. Liquid makes the bread mixable and creates steam. Are you creating steam or friction in a particular person's life right now? Do you want to change your behavior? If so, how could you begin to act more constructively to honor both yourself and the other person? Make a few notes for yourself.

Step 6: Adding lemon or almond extract. The extract adds the favor, the liveliness, the zip in this bread. In what ways are you sharing your liveliness or God-given gifts with others? Discuss.

Step 7: Adding flour. Flour is the mainstay of bread in every culture. Flour is found in the homes of rich and poor alike. There is a humble, dependable quality about flour which generates food for common people. How are you dependable? How are you, like flour, a mainstay in the lives of those around you? Discuss.

Step 8: Adding sugar. In a recipe for bread, the sugar serves as a catalyst for the yeast or baking powder. It feeds the baking powder and stimulates it and empowers it. How might you be a catalyst or an empowering agent for the people around you? Discuss.

Step 9: Adding poppy seed. Listen to the following brief verse discovered on a post in the middle of a garden:

Who plants a seed
Beneath the sod
And waits to see
Believes in God.

What seeds has God planted in you? Are they bearing fruit? Make a few notes to yourself.

Step 10: Adding baking powder. In this recipe, baking powder serves as the leaven or rising agent. Are you being what God created you to be? Are you rising to your God-given potential? Who or what in your life is your encourager or rising agent right now? Discuss.

Step 11: Shaping the loaf. As we pour the batter into the pan, we shape the loaf. Think of all the roles you play in your life. What opportunities do you have to shape those around you? How would you like to see this happen? What influences and values have shaped you? Discuss.

Put the bread in the oven to bake. Remove the loaves baked ahead of time, cut, talk, enjoy! Savor the aroma of what is in the oven as you take pleasure in the taste of the loaves already made.

TWENTY-ONE

THEME

Just as a snake sheds its old skin and embraces the newness of life, this culinary interlude invites our openness to change and growth.

I am indebted to Barbara Walker for the title "Eating the Serpent," and for the idea of preparing coiled bread.[1]

REFLECTING TOGETHER: OPPORTUNITIES FOR DISCUSSION

(The leader selects those topics and activities that are most appropriate for the group and for which there is time.)

An Opening Poem
To help establish the theme, the leader or a volunteer reads the following poem by Betsy James.

Snake Shedding

Skin dry and too tight,
eyes cloudy,
a snake lies in the May sun.

It is in vision that the change begins:
a fine line
creeps through the center of the world,
a crack that can widen.

The snake convulses.
The thin, dry membrane splits,
pulls back from the cornea
and curls away, unzipping
down the length of the back.

When the new, soft serpent
coils out in her painted hide,
her eyes are clear.[2]

Embracing Change

When the snake slips out of its old skin (usually in one piece), its identity is changed. It must shed its skin to accommodate its new growth. This usually happens several times each year. Thus, the snake can be for us a symbol of change.

Look over your life. What major changes or dramatic turning points have occurred? Did you choose them or did they just happen? How was your life different each time one of these changes took place?

Are you experiencing a period of change or a turning point in your life right now? What opportunities for growth might be revealed here for you? Discuss.

What changes would you like to see take place in your life? How might this happen? What might the timeline be for these changes? What steps could you take? Talk together.

Shedding

A snake's first shedding takes place shortly after it is hatched. A snake sheds its skin to give it more room to grow. In order to start the removal of its old skin, the snake assumes an active role and rubs its head or chin against a rough rock or a sharp branch. As the snake continues rubbing, the skin loosens around the head and then begins to split. The snake crawls out of its skin, turning it inside out, and slithers away wearing a new one.

In order to get where any of us are today, we have all had to shed the old and become reconciled to the new in one way or another. What have you intentionally shed in the past? How did that process go? What were the joyful aspects? What were the painful parts? At what points in your life did these times of shedding take place? Discuss.

The snake takes an active role in getting rid of its outgrown skin. What do you need to shed in order for your life to be the way you would like it to be? Are you assuming an active role in this process? Share your ideas.

FOOD AS SYMBOL

The suggested food for this occasion is either a large snake-shaped coiled bread that will serve the whole table or individual snake-shaped coiled breads.

Since "Eating the Serpent" can be planned for a morning coffee break, teatime, dessert, after dinner, etc., your choice of dough will depend on the time of day and the type of food the snake will be. Any heavy, dense bread will do: sweet bread or sweet roll dough, stollen dough with fruit and nuts, even cookie dough. If you're in a hurry, consider frozen bread dough or prepared sugar cookie dough. If you're fixing individual snakes, prepared breadstick dough, sold in a can, will do just fine.

Roll the dough into a long cylinder and then coil it to resemble a snake. To encourage group participation, each person could make his or her own snake and then chat while the dough is baking. If you are feeling really creative, decorate the snakes by scoring patterns in the dough to create "skin," or get wildly imaginative with some thin frosting and dribble it all over the snakes to create scale patterns. Decorating the snakes together will bring out the playful spirit in everyone.

TWENTY-TWO

THEME

This culinary interlude summons us to claim our own giftedness and our own unique purpose on earth.

REFLECTING TOGETHER

On a blank piece of paper, each person draws a picture of a big gift box which fills up the whole page.

The Bible reminds us in Ephesians 2:10 (MLB) that "we are [God's] handiwork." Yes, we are God's handiwork! You are a precious gift to the world and to those around you. Nobody else has been created quite like you. Answer the following questions by writing some notes inside the big gift box you have drawn:

1. For what purpose did God put you on earth?
2. What have you done in your life that best demonstrates what you believe?
3. What qualities as a woman or as a man do you bring to your creativity, your relationships, your spiritual community?
4. What are you striving to become or to be?

After you have had enough time to consider these questions thoughtfully, split up into groups of three or four to talk. One person in each group lights a large white candle which he or she explains as representing the creating spirit of God. This person then hands out small candles (birthday candles will do, or you can get inexpensive long, skinny tapers from any

141

party shop) and invites the members of the group to light their small candles individually in the flame of the larger one.

As each person lights a candle, those who wish to may share, in a sentence or two, what gift they would ask the creating spirit of God to nurture in them during the coming year. Each person then places his or her small candle on the "You Who Are the Gift Cake." (See "Food as Symbol.")

When all candles have been lighted and are on the cake, everyone holds hands and gathers in a circle around the glowing cake. The group sings the following song twice, to the tune of "Amazing Grace":

My gifts for God are rich indeed,
Unique to me alone.
God's call and purpose forward lead,
Through me God's seeds are sown.

Cut the cake and eat!

FOOD AS SYMBOL

The suggested food is a baked and frosted "You Who Are the Gift Cake." This culinary interlude can be planned for any time of the day. Vary your choice of cake accordingly: morning coffee cake, elegant dessert cake, etc. Remove the cake from the pan; frost in one color, draw ribbons with another color to make the cake look like a wrapped gift. If you're in a hurry, just buy a cake and stick on one of those flashy ready-made bows. The idea is to make the cake look as much like a wrapped gift as possible.

Appendix
SETTING THE TABLE AND CREATING THE ENVIRONMENT

When I get fired up about having friends over and preparing a meal, it's the thought of all those people searching out one another's lives and stories that gets me excited. There is nothing more satisfying to one who hosts a meal than to see guests offering one another their full attention as they talk and eat and talk some more.

SOME THOUGHTS ON SETTING THE SCENE

Provide a welcoming environment. Neatness, formality, sumptuousness are not very important, but a *welcoming environment* is. Here are some suggestions:

- ∾ Put your guests at ease.
- ∾ Do all the preparations you can ahead of time so you can visit.
- ∾ Ask for help. The best meals and parties are those in which everyone feels included and the glory is shared.
- ∾ Enjoy yourself. If you're uptight, everyone will feel the tension.
- ∾ Relax and let go.

I took a course in neurolinguistic programming (NLP) and learned that all of us receive sensory information in different ways. Some of us acquire information more strongly through our eyes, some of us more through touch, some of us more through taste or smell, some of us more strongly through our ears.

We must not assume that our preferred ways of absorbing data are the preferred and natural ways of others. I am very visual, gustatory, and olfactory. I am best at remembering scenes and tastes and smells. I have to be aware, however, that others I may be feasting with are more keenly aware of sounds or the sense of touch. When planning a gathering with food, try to incorporate as many sources of sensory input as possible so that everyone will receive sensory stimulation of one kind or another. In planning feasts, try to involve all the senses you can. Review the sensory checklist: seeing, hearing, tasting, smelling, touching.

HAND WASHING

An exceptionally civilized custom is hand washing before a ritualized and formal feast. I like the servanthood theology and the tender use of touch as well.

> *A hand-washing ceremony precedes formal meals in Botswana. Two women, sometimes younger girls, move from guest to guest. One carries a pitcher of water and the other carries a basin and a towel. They pour water over each guest's hands into the basin and offer a towel for drying.[1]*

Before a more formal meal, two children, perhaps one of each sex, might be asked to carry a bowl of water and a towel (a pitcher if desired) from guest to guest as is done in Botswana. The same ritual with the same or a different set of children might take place after the meal. Hand washing either before or after eating provides a convenient opportunity for the host, hostess, or leader to issue a welcome, an introduction to the theme of the meal, or afterwards to let the guests know what will happen next. Hand washing is the ultimate symbol of courtesy and hospitality.

If the pitcher-and-bowl kind of hand washing does not seem quite your style, another elegant after-dinner touch is the use of individual finger bowls. Each guest may receive a small bowl containing warm water and a slice of lemon. This is luxurious and comfortable and provides a transition into the celebration's next phase.

CANDLES

Candles provide warmth and light, and scented candles provide smell. Here are some suggestions for using candles.

Try placing votive candles in little glasses in as many safe locations as you can think of: in the middle of the table, one at each place, on the mantle, etc. How about filling a colorful bowl with white sand for summer or Epsom salt for winter and poking the votive candles down in? If that's too much trouble, white rice looks fine, too.

Luminarias are lovely at any time of the year and can be placed leading up to a front door, or—if there are no children running around—down a hallway. They are charming sitting on bookshelves or anywhere else. Open a lunch-sized paper bag, put sand in the bottom, and stick in an inexpensive plumber's candle.

Try placing candlesticks of various heights and combinations anywhere you like. Do make sure that overly tall candlesticks in the middle of the dining table don't prevent guests from looking into one another's faces.

A scented candle safely contained and burning cozily is especially welcoming in the front hall or bathroom.

GOOD SMELLS

People love to enter a kitchen that smells good. If a hot meal is being prepared, the enticing aroma from oven or crockpot may be enough. Other good sources of aromatherapy include the following.

Hot Bread

Hot bread is delicious almost any day of the year except for the warmest summer days. If you don't have time to enter into the calming process of real yeast bread making, then try some easy recipes for beer bread, baking powder quick breads, or corn bread. Or if you have access to a bread machine, put the ingredients in, set the timer, and have the bread ready to pull out at just the right moment. Ahh. What a treat!

Hot Cider

Almost any feast I prepare in the fall or winter is preceded by hot cider. When folks walk in, they can smell those cinnamon sticks and that apple juice brewing together. If you like to make hot cider in a big pot on the stove, a couple of whole apples with cloves stuck in them enhance the flavor and look pretty bobbing around.

Simmering Scents

If you can't find anything to actually eat that will arouse your guests' noses and get their tongues hanging out, you can always simmer something in a saucepan by itself. (This is also good if you're selling your house and prospective buyers are traipsing in.) One such recipe follows.

Peel of one whole orange, cut up
Peel of one whole lemon, cut up
3 cinnamon sticks
8 cloves
2 cups water

Combine in a saucepan and simmer. If the water gets too low, add some more.

If you're really short of time, just put a couple of tablespoons of ground cinnamon in a saucepan with several cups of water and simmer.

MUSIC

Music is soothing and should always be played only as background. Be sure your guests can talk comfortably. Choose selections that will appeal to almost everyone's taste.

SPARKLERS

Sparklers are extraordinarily festive and inexpensive. Stock up at half-price July 5 sales. Stick them in cakes or hand them out.

CENTERPIECES

Centerpieces can be displayed on your dining table if there is still room for the food, or they can be placed on other eye-catching surfaces as well. Some ideas:

- ∾ *Pots, bowls, bouquets of flowers:*
  Don't run out and buy fancy containers if you don't already have them. A glass or a pitcher makes a nice vase.
- ∾ *Baskets or colorful bowls of fresh fruits or vegetables:*
  I like cloves in a lot of things. Clove-studded lemons, limes, or oranges smell delicious.
- ∾ *Collections:*
  Do you collect something? shells? rocks? figurines? feathers? Collections of small objects can make unusual centerpieces and enlivening conversation starters as well.

FABRIC

It's amazing what a little fabric will do. Even a homey, clean kitchen towel with a few candles and vegetables makes a captivating centerpiece. Maybe you're into silk scarves, lace, or bandannas. Some of my most becoming table runners are long, flowing scarves I discovered in my bedroom drawer. And how about lamé? I confess I'm a bit of a lamé addict. The turquoise-green lamés look like the Caribbean. Cruise the aisles of your local fabric store. Even the smallest amount of your favorite cloth enhances a centerpiece and the feast.

TABLECLOTHS

Tablecloths don't have to be traditional. Try a remnant you like or a designer sheet, an afghan, a rug, or a bedspread. (When we serve curry at our house, I always put the cotton Indian bedspread from college days on the table.) Remember, use something you feel relaxed about. There's no reason to take a guest's head off for spilling.

PLACECARDS

Placecards add a welcoming touch and make every guest feel known and remembered. Interior designer Alexandra Stoddard suggests putting guests' names on both sides of the card so that the friend across the table can see the name, too. Children are clever at making placecards and like to be included in the preparations. For simple placecards, trace around cookie cutters to draw shapes; use glitter pens or stickers; glue on ribbons or dried flowers.

GOBLETS

I am not going to launch into a whole section on servingware, but I do have to mention goblets because they transform the simplest of concoctions into something elegant. Part of my lunch just now was a carton of yogurt and some raspberries from our backyard. I poured it all into a tall goblet and found myself savoring my lunch rather than gulping it down. Goblets make the simplest drink look refined, including water. (A lemon slice in the ice water does add panache.) For an especially fancy feast, tie ribbons around the stems of your goblets. Goblets need not be crystal (unless you really want them to sing) and they need not be expensive. We have a number of bulk discount stores in our area, and when they have glamorous goblets I stock up. Some tasty foods to serve in goblets include cold summer fruit or vegetable soup, ice cream drinks or milkshakes, scoops of ice cream or sundaes, fruit salad, sherbet or sorbet. Here is a favorite quick dessert to serve in goblets:

> Scoop two scoops of pineapple sherbet into each glass. Thin raspberry preserves with orange juice. Spoon over sherbet. Refreshing!

ROUND TWO

I find that folks often appreciate, as Winnie the Pooh would say, "a little smackerel of something" about two hours after dinner. Perhaps there's a little more dessert to pass around. Maybe there are some after-dinner mints, a munchie mix, or fruit and cheese. Pour coffee, tea, hot chocolate, seltzer water, soda—whatever seems to be appreciated by your guests. A small round two is not at all necessary but adds a graceful touch.

Notes

INTRODUCTION

1. Brother Peter Reinhart, *Sacramental Magic in a Small-Town Café* (Reading, Mass.: Addison-Wesley, 1994), xxii–xxiii.
2. Sarah Hall Maney, "Cooking: Divine and Destructive," in *Sacred Dimensions of Women's Experience*, ed. Elizabeth Dodson Gray (Wellesley, Mass.: Roundtable Press, 1988), 173.
3. M. F. K. Fisher, *The Art of Eating* (New York: Collier Books, Macmillan Publishing Company, 1937), 353.
4. Sharon Parks, "The Meaning of Eating and the Home as Ritual Space," in *Sacred Dimensions of Women's Experience*, 185.
5. Matthew Fox, *Original Blessing* (Santa Fe: Bear & Company, 1983), 112–13.
6. Walter Brueggemann, *Genesis* (Atlanta: John Knox Press, 1982), 39.
7. Tilden Edwards, *Living in the Presence: Disciplines for the Spiritual Heart* (San Francisco: Harper & Row, 1987), 31.
8. Kelton Cobb, "Table Blessings," *The Christian Century* (5 March 1986): 242.
9. Joetta Handrich Schlabach, *Extending the Table* (Scottdale, Pa.: Herald Press, 1991), 179.

1. BRINGING HEAVEN TO EARTH

1. *An Inclusive Language Lectionary: Readings for Year A* (Atlanta: John Knox Press; New York: The Pilgrim Press; Philadelphia: Westminster Press, 1983), reading for Pentecost 21.
2. Sara Covin Juengst, *Breaking Bread: The Spiritual Significance of Food* (Louisville: Westminster John Knox, 1992), 84–85.

3. Gabriele Uhlein, trans., *Meditations with Hildegard of Bingen* (Santa Fe: Bear & Company, 1983), 128.

4. The idea for "Rules for Changing the World" comes from Barbara G. Walker, *Women's Rituals: A Sourcebook* (San Francisco: Harper & Row, 1990), 88.

5. Ibid.

6. *An Inclusive Language Lectionary: Readings for Year B* (Atlanta: John Knox Press; New York: The Pilgrim Press; Philadelphia: The Westminster Press, rev. ed., 1987), 144.

7. Judy Chicago, *The Dinner Party: A Symbol of Our Heritage* (Garden City, N.Y.: Anchor Press/Doubleday, 1979), 256.

8. Juengst, *Breaking Bread*, 91.

2. TABLE OF CREATIVITY

1. Joseph Chilton Pearce, quoted in Julia Cameron, *The Artist's Way: A Spiritual Path to Higher Creativity* (New York: Jeremy P. Tarcher/Perigee Books, 1992), 2.

2. Madeleine L'Engle, quoted in Nena Bryans, *Full Circle: A Proposal to the Church for an Arts Ministry* (San Carlos, Calif.: Schuyler Institute for Worship and the Arts, 1988), 51.

3. Matthew Fox, trans., *Meditations with Meister Eckhart* (Santa Fe: Bear & Company, 1983), 88.

4. Martha Graham, quoted in Cameron, *The Artist's Way*, 75.

5. Maria Harris, *Dance of the Spirit: The Seven Steps of Women's Spirituality* (New York: Bantam Books, 1989), 129.

6. Dorothee Soelle with Shirley A. Cloyes, *To Work and to Love: A Theology of Creation* (Philadelphia: Fortress Press, 1984), 96.

7. Helena Matheopoulos, *Maestro: Encounters with Conductors of Today* (New York: Harper & Row, 1982), 11.

8. Kay Leigh Hagan, *Prayers to the Moon: Exercises in Self-Reflection* (San Francisco: HarperSanFrancisco, 1991), 124.

3. BOAST, TOAST, AND BOAST SOME MORE

1. Idea adapted from Starhawk, *Truth or Dare: Encounters with Power, Authority, and Mystery* (San Francisco: Harper & Row, 1987), 136.

4. RITES OF PASSAGE: A FEAST OF NEW BEGINNINGS

1. May Sarton, *At Seventy: A Journal* (New York: W. W. Norton, 1984), 10.
2. Ignatius of Loyola, in Thomas H. Green, *Weeds Among the Wheat* (Notre Dame, Ind.: Ave Maria Press, 1984), 86.

5. FLAMBOYANT FANTASY: AN OUTRAGEOUS FEAST

1. The idea of creating an outrageous feast is inspired by Maria Harris, *Teaching and Religious Imagination: An Essay in the Theology of Teaching* (San Francisco: Harper & Row, 1987), 179–80.
2. Gloria Steinem, *Outrageous Acts and Everyday Rebellions* (New York: New American Library, 1983), 355–56.
3. Jim Fowler and Sam Keen, *Life Maps: Conversations on the Journey of Faith* (Waco, Tex.: Word Books, 1978), 120–21.
4. Cameron, *The Artist's Way*, 148.

6. BROADENING THE BOUNDARIES: A GLOBAL POTLUCK

1. The idea of hospitality as a holy duty is taken from Juengst, *Breaking Bread*, 37.
2. Henri J. M. Nouwen, *Reaching Out: The Three Movements of the Spiritual Life* (New York: Doubleday, 1975), 66.
3. Vincent Kavaloski, "What Is the Middle East in the Middle Of?" *Metanoia: Newsletter of the Ecumenical Partnership for Peace and Justice of the Wisconsin Conference of Churches* (summer 1991): 2.
4. Schlabach, *Extending the Table*, 29.
5. Nouwen, *Reaching Out*, 65.
6. In composing this guided imagery, I was inspired by Carolyn Stahl Bohler, *Prayer on Wings: A Search for Authentic Prayer* (San Diego: LuraMedia, 1990), 105.
7. Joseph Campbell with Bill Moyers, *The Power of Myth* (New York: Doubleday, 1988), 32.

7. TAKING CARE: A FEAST OF COMFORT

1. This idea is adapted from Starhawk, *Truth or Dare: Encounters with Power, Authority, and Mystery* (San Francisco: Harper & Row, 1987), 235.
2. Jennifer Louden calls this a "magic question" in *The Women's Comfort Book: A Self-Nurturing Guide for Restoring Balance in Your Life* (San Francisco: HarperSanFrancisco, 1992), 8.
3. Hagan, *Prayers to the Moon*, 80.
4. Ibid., 28.

5. Adapted from Lucia Capacchione, *The Creative Journal: The Art of Finding Yourself* (North Hollywood, Calif.: Newcastle Publishing, 1989), 94.

8. AT WISDOM'S TABLE

1. Susan Cady, Marian Ronan, and Hal Taussig, *Wisdom's Feast: Sophia in Study and Celebration* (San Francisco: Harper & Row, 1989), 94.
2. Ibid., 99.
3. Roger Rosenblatt, "Where in the World . . . ," *Family Circle*, June 8, 1993, 152.
4. The idea of drawing a map with thus described obstacles and helpers is taken from Capacchione, *The Creative Journal,* 172.
5. Eleanor S. Morrison, *Honoring the Gifts of Wisdom and Age* (Lansing, Mich.: Leaven, Inc., 1993), 32.
6. Adapted from Morrison, *Honoring the Gifts of Wisdom and Age,* 25–26.

9. FEAST OF WONDER

1. *Inclusive Language Psalms* (New York: The Pilgrim Press, 1987), 35.
2. E. E. Cummings, *100 Selected Poems* (New York: Grove Press, 1923), 114.
3. Fox, trans., *Meditations with Meister Eckhart,* 33.
4. Cameron, *The Artist's Way,* 53.
5. The idea to write such a guided imagery was inspired by Harris, *Dance of the Spirit,* 50–51.
6. Flora Slosson Wuellner, *Prayer and Our Bodies* (Nashville: The Upper Room, 1987), 60.

10. CELEBRATION FOR A CHOSEN FAMILY

1. Christina Baldwin, *Life's Companion: Journal Writing as a Spiritual Quest* (New York: Bantam Books, 1990), 316.
2. Marie Livingston Roy, "Not Servants," *Alive Now!* (Jan./Feb. 1984): 43.
3. Sherry Ruth Anderson and Patricia Hopkins, *The Feminine Face of God* (New York: Bantam Books, 1991), 200.
4. Cathleen Rountree, *Coming Into Our Fullness: On Women Turning Forty* (Freedom, Calif.: The Crossing Press, 1991), 190.

11. EVERYONE WORKING TOGETHER

1. Marcia Brown, *Stone Soup* (New York: Scribner, 1947).

12. BIRTHDAY FEAST

1. The idea of the life story circle comes from Sedonia Cahill and Joshua Halpern, *The Ceremonial Circle: Practice, Ritual, and Renewal for Personal and Community Healing* (San Francisco: HarperSanFrancisco, 1990), 144–45.
2. Fox, trans., *Meditations with Meister Eckhart*, 32.
3. Anthony Bloom, *Beginning to Pray* (New York: Paulist Press, 1970), 49–50.

13. LIVING IN THANKSGIVING: A FEAST OF GRATITUDE

1. Baldwin, *Life's Companion*, 343.
2. Ibid., 232.
3. Ibid., 184.
4. Hagan, *Prayers to the Moon*, 160.

14. NATURE'S BOUNTY: A SUMMER PICNIC

1. The ideas for "Smells of Summer" comes from Nancy Brady Cunningham, *Feeding the Spirit: How to Create Your Own Ceremonial Rites, Festivals, and Celebrations* (San Jose, Calif.: Resource Publications, 1988), 92–93.
2. Mary C. Coelho, "Understanding Consolation and Desolation," *Review for Religious* (Jan.–Feb. 1985): 74–75.
3. Baldwin, *Life's Companion*, 328.
4. Ibid.
5. Edwards, *Living in the Presence*, 23–24.
6. Fox, trans., *Meditations with Meister Eckhart*, 14.
7. John Muir, quoted in Joseph Cornell, *Listening to Nature* (Nevada City, Calif.: Dawn Publications, 1987), 66.
8. Bonnie Bernstein, ed., *Concoctions* (Palo Alto, Calif.: Monday Morning Books, 1987), 54, 52.

15. TRUSTING AND WAITING: A WINTER PICNIC

1. Harris, *Dance of the Spirit*, 195.
2. Elizabeth Roberts and Elias Amidon, eds., *Earth Prayers from Around the World: 365 Prayers, Poems, and Invocations for Honoring the Earth* (San Francisco: HarperSanFrancisco, 1991), 288.
3. Fox, trans., *Meditations with Meister Eckhart*, 28.

16. FEAST OF THE FOREMOTHERS

1. Kathleen Fischer, *Women at the Well: Feminist Perspectives on Spiritual Direction* (Mahwah, N.J.: Paulist Press, 1988), 196.
2. Naomi Ruth Lowinsky, *Stories from the Motherline: Reclaiming the Mother-Daughter Bond, Finding Our Feminine Souls* (Los Angeles: Jeremy P. Tarcher, 1992), 12.
3. This method of introducing mothers and daughters is from Lowinsky, *Stories from the Motherline*, 11.
4. "Standing before Us" may be ordered from Carole Etzler Eagleheart, Sisters Unlimited, RR#1, Box 1420, Bridport, VT 05734.
5. Harris, *Dance of the Spirit*, 141.
6. The idea of telling a grandmother story is from Lowinsky, Stories from the Motherline, 214.
7. "Womanriver Flowing On" may be ordered from Carole Etzler Eagleheart, Sisters Unlimited, RR#1, Box 1420, Bridport, VT 05734.

17. TEA AND SABBATH

1. Gray, *Sacred Dimension of Women's Experience*, 150.
2. Daisetz T. Suzuki, *Zen and Japanese Culture* (New York: Pantheon Books, 1959), 283, 314.

3. *An Inclusive-Language Lectionary: Readings for Year B*, 83.
4. Harris, *Dance of the Spirit*, 93.
5. Molly Cone, *The Jewish Sabbath* (New York: Thomas Y. Crowell, 1966), n.p.
6. Abraham Joshua Heschel, *The Sabbath: Its Meaning for Modern Man* (New York: Farrar, Straus & Giroux, 1951).
7. Marjorie J. Thompson, *Family—The Forming Center: A Vision of the Role of Family in Spiritual Formation* (Nashville: Upper Room Books, 1989), 71.

18. HEARTS!

1. Edward Hays, *Prayers for a Planetary Pilgrim: A Personal Manual for Prayer and Ritual* (Easton, Kans.: Forest of Peace Books, 1988), 64.
2. Harris, *Dance of the Spirit*, 36.
3. Antoine de Saint-Exupéry, *The Little Prince* (New York: Harcourt Brace Jovanovich, 1943), 70.
4. Kenneth Leech, *True Prayer: An Invitation to Christian Spirituality* (San Francisco: Harper & Row, 1980), 40.
5. The idea for this "art as meditation" comes from Madeline McMurray, *Illuminations: The Healing Image* (Berkeley, Calif.: Wingbow Press, 1988), 35.

19. EATING ON THE MOUNTAINTOP

1. Martin Luther King Jr., *I Have a Dream: Writings and Speeches That Changed the World* (San Francisco: HarperSanFrancisco, 1986), 203.
2. Ram Dass, *Journey of Awakening: A Meditator's Guidebook* (New York: Bantam Books, 1978), 211.
3. Baldwin, *Life's Companion*, 232.

2 0 . M A K I N G A N D B R E A K I N G B R E A D

1. Darlene Christiansen, "Hands in Ministry: Baking and Breaking Bread," *Common Lot* (winter 1989): 26–28.

2 1 . E A T I N G T H E S E R P E N T

1. See "Eating the Serpent" in Walker, *Women's Rituals*, 183–85.

A P P E N D I X : S E T T I N G T H E T A B L E A N D C R E A T I N G T H E E N V I R O N M E N T

1. Schlabach, *Extending the Table*, 240.

SELECTED BIBLIOGRAPHY

Anderson, Sherry Ruth, and Patricia Hopkins. *The Feminine Face of God*. New York: Bantam Books, 1991.

Baldwin, Christina. *Life's Companion: Journal Writing as a Spiritual Quest*. New York: Bantam Books, 1990.

Bateson, Mary Catherine. *Composing a Life*. New York: Plume, 1990.

Beck, Renee, and Sydney Barbara Metrick. *The Art of Ritual: A Guide to Creating and Performing Your Own Rituals for Growth and Change*. Berkeley, Calif.: Celestial Arts, 1990.

Belenky, Mary Field, Blythe McVicker Clinchy, Nancy Rule Goldberger, and Jill Mattuck Tarule. *Women's Ways of Knowing: The Development of Self, Voice, and Mind*. New York: Basic Books, 1986.

Bernstein, Bonnie, ed. *Concoctions*. Palo Alto, Calif.: Monday Morning Books, 1987.

Bloom, Anthony. *Beginning to Pray*. New York: Paulist Press, 1970.

Bohler, Carolyn Stahl. *Prayer on Wings: A Search for Authentic Prayer*. San Diego: LuraMedia, 1990.

Broner, E. M. *The Telling: The Story of a Group of Jewish Women Who Journey to Spirituality through Community and Ceremony*. San Francisco: HarperSanFrancisco, 1993.

Brown, Marcia. *Stone Soup*. New York: Scribner, 1947.

Brueggemann, Walter. *Genesis*. Atlanta: John Knox Press, 1982.

Bryans, Nena. *Full Circle: A Proposal to the Church for an Arts Ministry*. San Carlos, Calif.: Schuyler Institute for Worship and the Arts, 1988.

Cady, Susan, Marian Ronan, and Hal Taussig. *Wisdom's Feast: Sophia in Study and Celebration*. San Francisco: Harper & Row, 1989.

Cahill, Sedonia, and Joshua Halpern. *The Ceremonial Circle: Practice, Ritual, and Renewal for Personal and Community Healing*. San Francisco: HarperSanFrancisco, 1990.

Cameron, Julia. *The Artist's Way: A Spiritual Path to Higher Creativity.* New York: Jeremy P. Tarcher/Perigee, 1992.

Campbell, Joseph, with Bill Moyers. *The Power of Myth.* New York: Doubleday, 1988.

Capacchione, Lucia. *The Creative Journal: The Art of Finding Yourself.* North Hollywood, Calif.: Newcastle, 1989.

Chicago, Judy. *The Dinner Party: A Symbol of Our Heritage.* Garden City, N.Y.: Anchor Press/Doubleday, 1979.

Christiansen, Darlene. "Hands in Ministry: Baking and Breaking Bread." *Common Lot* (winter 1989): 26–28.

Clarke, Thomas. "On the Need to Break Bread Together." In *Human Rights in the Americas: The Struggle for Consensus,* edited by Alfred Hennelly and John Langan. Washington, D.C.: Georgetown University Press, 1982.

Coelho, Mary C. "Understanding Consolation and Desolation." *Review for Religious* (Jan.–Feb. 1985): 61–77.

Cone, Molly. *The Jewish Sabbath.* New York: Thomas Y. Crowell, 1966.

Cornell, Joseph. *Listening to Nature.* Nevada City, Calif.: Dawn Publications, 1987.

Cummings, E. E. *100 Selected Poems.* New York: Grove Press, 1923.

Cunningham, Nancy Brady. *Feeding the Spirit: How to Create Your Own Ceremonial Rites, Festivals, and Celebrations.* San Jose, Calif.: Resource Publications, 1988.

Duerk, Judith. *Circle of Stones: Woman's Journey to Herself.* San Diego: LuraMedia, 1989.

Durka, Gloria. *Praying with Hildegard of Bingen.* Winona, Minn.: St, Mary's Press, 1991.

Edwards, Tilden. *Living in the Presence: Disciplines for the Spiritual Heart.* San Francisco: Harper & Row, 1987.

Ferrucci, Piero. *Inevitable Grace.* Los Angeles: Jeremy P. Tarcher, 1990.

Fischer, Kathleen. *Women at the Well: Feminist Perspectives on Spiritual Direction.* Mahwah, N.J.: Paulist Press, 1988.

Fisher, M. F. K. *The Art of Eating.* New York: Collier Books, Macmillan, 1937.

Fowler, Jim, and Sam Keen. *Life Maps: Conversations on the Journey of Faith*. Waco, Tex.: Word Books, 1978.

Fox, Matthew, trans. *Meditations with Meister Eckhart*. Santa Fe: Bear & Company, 1983.

    Original Blessing. Santa Fe: Bear & Company, 1983.

Gray, Elizabeth Dodson, ed. *Sacred Dimensions of Women's Experience*. Wellesley, Mass.: Roundtable Press, 1988.

Green, Thomas H. *Weeds Among the Wheat*. Notre Dame, Ind.: Ave Maria Press, 1984.

Hagan, Kay Leigh. *Prayers to the Moon: Exercises in Self-Reflection*. San Francisco: HarperSanFrancisco, 1991.

Harris, Maria. *Dance of the Spirit: The Seven Steps of Women's Spirituality*. New York: Bantam Books, 1989.

————. *Jubilee Time: Celebrating Women, Spirit, and the Advent of Age*. New York: Bantam Books, 1995.

————. *Teaching and Religious Imagination: An Essay in the Theology of Teaching*. San Francisco: Harper & Row,, 1987.

Hays, Edward. *Prayers for a Planetary Pilgrim: A Personal Manual for Prayer and Ritual*. Easton, Kans.: Forest of Peace Books, 1988.

Heschel, Abraham Joshua. *The Sabbath: Its Meaning for Modern Man*. New York: Farrar, Straus & Giroux, 1951.

An Inclusive Language Lectionary: Readings for Year A. Atlanta: John Knox Press; New York: The Pilgrim Press; Philadelphia: The Westminster Press, 1983.

An Inclusive-Language Lectionary: Readings for Year B. Atlanta: John Knox Press; New York: The Pilgrim Press; Philadelphia: The Westminster Press, 1987.

Juengst, Sara Covin. *Breaking Bread: The Spiritual Significance of Food*. Louisville: Westminster John Knox, 1992.

Keen, Sam, and Anne Valley-Fox. *Your Mythic Journey: Finding Meaning in Your Life through Writing and Storytelling*. Los Angeles: Jeremy P. Tarcher, 1973.

King, Martin Luther, Jr. *I Have a Dream: Writings and Speeches That Changed the World.* San Francisco: HarperSanFrancisco, 1986.

Leech, Kenneth. *True Prayer: An Invitation to Christian Spirituality.* San Francisco: Harper & Row, 1980.

Longacre, Doris Janzen. *More-with-Less Cookbook.* Scottdale, Pa.: Herald Press, 1976.

Louden, Jennifer. *The Women's Comfort Book: A Self-Nurturing Guide for Restoring Balance in Your Life.* San Francisco: HarperSanFrancisco, 1992.

Lowinsky, Naomi Ruth. *Stories from the Motherline: Reclaiming the Mother-Daughter Bond, Finding Our Feminine Souls.* Los Angeles: Jeremy P. Tarcher, 1992.

Matheopoulos, Helena. *Maestro: Encounters with Conductors of Today.* New York: Harper & Row, 1982.

McMakin, Jacqueline with Rhoda Nary. *Doorways to Christian Growth.* San Francisco: Harper & Row, 1984.

McMakin, Jacqueline, with Sonya Dyer. *Working from the Heart.* San Francisco: LuraMedia, 1989.

McMurray, Madeline. *Illuminations: The Healing Image.* Berkeley, Calif.: Wingbow Press, 1988.

Morrison, Eleanor S. *Honoring the Gifts of Wisdom and Age.* Lansing, Mich.: Leaven, Inc., 1993.

Nouwen, Henri J. M. *Reaching Out: The Three Movements of the Spiritual Life.* New York: Doubleday, 1975.

Ram Dass. *Journey of Awakening: A Meditator's Guidebook.* New York: Bantam Books, 1978.

Reinhart, Brother Peter. *Sacramental Magic in a Small-Town Café.* Reading, Mass.: Addison-Wesley, 1994.

Roberts, Elizabeth, and Elias Amidon, eds. *Earth Prayers from Around the World: 365 Prayers, Poems, and Invocations for Honoring the Earth.* San Francisco: HarperSanFrancisco, 1991.

Rosenblatt, Roger. "Where in the World . . . ," *Family Circle,* 8 June 1993.

Roy, Marie Livingston. "Not Servants." *Alive Now!* Jan./Feb. 1984.

Rountree, Cathleen. *Coming into Our Fullness: On Women Turning Forty.* Freedom, Calif.: The Crossing Press, 1991.

Rupp, Joyce. *May I Have This Dance?* Notre Dame, Ind.: Ave Maria Press, 1992.

Saint-Exupéry, Antoine de. *The Little Prince.* New York: Harcourt Brace Jovanovich, 1943.

Sanford, Linda Tschirhart, and Mary Ellen Donovan. *Women and Self-Esteem: Understanding and Improving the Way We Think and Feel about Ourselves.* New York: Penguin Books, 1984.

Sarton, May. *At Seventy: A Journal.* New York: W. W. Norton, 1984.

Schlabach, Joetta Handrich. *Extending the Table.* Scottdale, Pa.: Herald Press, 1991.

Soelle, Dorothee, with Shirley A. Cloyes. *To Work and to Love: A Theology of Creation.* Philadelphia: Fortress Press, 1984.

Stahl, Carolyn. *Opening to God: Guided Imagery Meditation on Scripture for Individuals and Groups.* Nashville: The Upper Room, 1977.

Starhawk. *The Spiral Dance.* San Francisco: Harper & Row, 1979.

———. *Truth or Dare: Encounters with Power, Authority, and Mystery.* San Francisco: Harper & Row, 1987.

Steinem, Gloria. *Outrageous Acts and Everyday Rebellions.* New York: New American Library, 1983.

Suzuki, Daisetz T. *Zen and Japanese Culture.* New York: Pantheon Books, 1959.

Thompson, Marjorie J. *Family—The Forming Center: A Vision of the Role of Family in Spiritual Formation.* Nashville: Upper Room Books, 1989.

———. *Soul Feast: An Invitation to the Christian Life.* Louisville: Westminster John Knox, 1995.

Uhlein, Gabriele, trans. *Meditations with Hildegard of Bingen.* Santa Fe: Bear & Company, 1983.

Walker, Barbara G. *Women's Rituals: A Sourcebook.* San Francisco: Harper & Row, 1990.

Wuellner, Flora Slosson. *Prayer and Our Bodies.* Nashville: The Upper Room, 1987.

ABOUT THE AUTHOR

Holly Wilson Whitcomb has been a pastor and clergywoman in the United Church of Christ since her graduation from Yale Divinity School in 1978, and has served churches in Connecticut, Iowa, and Wisconsin. She is also a graduate of the two-year training program for spiritual directors at the Shalem Institute for Spiritual Formation in Bethesda, Maryland. Holly is a retreat leader, spiritual director, and workshop facilitator who travels to churches, retreat houses, and conference centers all over the country. As the founder of Kettlewood, a ministry of spiritual formation, she not only leads retreats, but also cooks for the guests who come to Kettlewood. She is a jewelry maker and fabric artist who frequently incorporates "art as meditation" into her spiritual work. A freelance writer, Holly has published more than forty resources in various books and periodicals. She lives in a suburb of Milwaukee, Wisconsin, with her husband, John, and their two children, David and Kate.

You may contact Holly Whitcomb by calling the Kettlewood office, (414) 784-5593, or by sending e-mail to ChotaWhit@aol.com.